Quality
Management
Plus

Quality
Management
Plus

The Continuous
Improvement of
Education

Roger Kaufman
Douglas Zahn

CORWIN PRESS, INC.
A Sage Publications Company
Newbury Park, California

For information address:

Corwin Press, Inc.
A Sage Publications Company
2455 Teller Road
Newbury Park, California 91320

SAGE Publications Ltd.
6 Bonhill Street
London EC2A 4PU
United Kingdom

SAGE Publications India Pvt. Ltd.
M-32 Market
Greater Kailash I
New Delhi 110 048 India

Printed in the United States of America

Library of Congress Cataloging-in-Publication Data

Kaufman, Roger
   Quality management plus: the continuous improvement of education / Roger Kaufman, Douglas Zahn.
      p. cm.
   Includes bibliographical references and index.
   ISBN 0-8039-6062-X
   1. School management and organization—United States. 2. Total quality management—United States. I. Zahn, Douglas, 1943–
II. Title.
LB2805.K37 1993   92-42929
371.2'00973—dc20   CIP

The paper in this book meets the specifications for permanence of the American National Standards Institute and the National Association of State Textbook Administrators.

93 94 95 96 10 9 8 7 6 5 4 3 2 1

Corwin Press Production Editor: Tara S. Mead

Contents

Preface

Little in our society has attracted more recent attention than education. It is vital to our survival, yet it is experiencing severe trouble meeting its assigned obligations. As cultural and ethnic diversity grows in our neighborhoods and schools, the design and delivery of useful education become more problematic. Educators and their partners are working harder and worrying more. But they are still under attack. Education can and must be helped to become successful.

Educators have not been shy about trying new things in the past. We have seen program after program and hot idea after hot idea piled onto educators. Not questioning what might be causing the problems in education, and how best to reverse its fortunes, educators and citizens alike are searching willy-nilly for ways to help develop successful citizens for tomorrow. They tinker, meddle, complain, restructure, reorganize, and legislate. Not meeting our challenge is not because of lack of intention or ill will.

Yet change we must. We don't want change for its own sake. We want to truly provide learning opportunities so that today's learners will become tomorrow's contributing citizens. These well-prepared future citizens will, in turn, fashion a better world for their children. But we never seem to find the right solutions to our lingering and often seemingly intractable problems.

It is time to get serious about defining and delivering educational quality. We have to get serious about defining what education must deliver and assure that we find the most effective and efficient ways to get the job done. When monies are short, it seems a bit ironic that the most practical ways to define and deliver educational success are not very expensive. In fact, their use will probably save both money and the anguish of failing our learners. What is the secret? Plan where education should head and what it must deliver (some call that *strategic planning*) and involve and empower everyone in assuring that quality is the hallmark of what is delivered (often termed *quality management*). When quality management and strategic planning are brought together, the impressive power of each is improved still more.

Quality management and continuous improvement—the topic of this book—are sensible, rational, and logical. They put the clients'—learners' and citizens'—success and well-being in central focus.

This book provides the "what's," "why's," and "how's" of quality management in education. We view it as a continuous process for defining and achieving added efficiency as well as defining and delivering new and continuing effectiveness.

This book is not about slogans, statistics, banners, and record keeping. It is about people, partnerships, purposes, accomplishment, science, and societal contribution. It is not a rehash of industrial models and concepts but builds upon the successes of the private sector, creating an approach specifically for education. It is based upon what can and will work in education. It provides what to do, when to do it, as well as procedures for hands-on application.

We go beyond conventional total quality management models and approaches, as good as they are. We add an additional dimension: success in and for tomorrow's world—helping create the world for tomorrow's child. This book is about QM for those who want to extend the reach and ramifications of educational success to society. It provides the added dimension of *quality management plus* (QM+).

Acknowledgments

We wish to express our appreciation to many people, who bear no responsibility for any problems in this final version, who helped make this book better than it would have been otherwise. Specifically, we thank Priscilla Broen (English teacher, Leon County, Florida), Frank Broen (Vice President, TeachAmerica Corporation), Bill Peterson (writer, Miami, Florida), P. George Benson (Associate Professor of Management, University of Minnesota), Dan Boroto (Associate Professor of Psychology, Florida State University), Andrea Zahn (colleague and supporter, Tallahassee, Florida), Jac Kaufman (WCTV, Tallahassee, Florida), Duane Meeter (Professor of Statistics, Florida State University), Mary Baggett (Manager, Statistical Consulting Center, Florida State University), Kathi Watters (Center for Needs Assessment and Planning, Florida State University), Phil Grisé (Center for Needs Assessment and Planning, Florida State University), Leon Sims (Center for Needs Assessment and Planning, Florida State University), Jan Kaufman (puppeteer), Atsusi Harumi (Center for Educational Technology, Florida State University), Hanna Mayer (performance systems and quality auditing consultant, Toronto, Canada), and literally hundreds of professional educators and learners of all ages who have made us continually improve.

We wish to express our appreciation to three publishers who allowed us to use and modify previously published material: Technomic Publications, Inc., for material from Kaufman's *Planning Educational Systems* and Kaufman and Herman's *Strategic Planning in Education*; Sage Publications for material from Kaufman's *Strategic Planning Plus*; and Corwin Press for content from Kaufman's *Mapping Educational Success*.

Our sincere thanks go to Gracia Alkema, President of Corwin Press, who thought this book important enough to bring to you.

Thanks also to Jason Strickland for assistance on graphics, and our thanks to the staff of Corwin Press, who always sought first to communicate and make a worthwhile contribution to the readers.

ROGER KAUFMAN
DOUGLAS ZAHN

About the Authors

Roger Kaufman is Professor and Director, Center for Needs Assessment and Planning, at Florida State University. He is also affiliated with the Department of Industrial Engineering and Management Systems at the University of Central Florida. Previously, he was Professor at the United States International University, Chapman University, and he also taught at the University of Southern California. His Ph.D. is from New York University, with graduate and undergraduate work in industrial engineering, psychology, communications, and education at the University of California (at Berkeley), Johns Hopkins, George Washington, and Purdue.

His work in the private sector has included the following: Assistant to the Vice President for Research, and Assistant to the Vice President for Engineering, at Douglas Aircraft Company; Director of Training System Analysis at US Industries; and head of human factors engineering at Martin Baltimore and earlier at Boeing. He has served two terms on the Secretary of the Navy's Advisory Board on

Education and Training and served as consultant to many private and public sector organizations covering every continent. He has worked with many school systems and school boards in the areas of strategic planning, needs assessment, management, and evaluation.

He is a fellow (educational psychology) of the American Psychological Association and a Diplomate (school psychology) of the American Board of Professional Psychology. He has been named "Member for Life" of the National Society for Performance & Instruction, an organization that he has served as president. He has published 25 books on strategic planning, needs assessment, management, and evaluation and is the author of more than 140 articles on those topics.

Douglas Zahn is Professor of Statistics at Florida State University. He is also on the staff of the Statistical Consulting Center at FSU. He has served as Visiting Associate Professor of Statistics at Harvard University. He earned his Ph.D. and A.M. (statistics) from Harvard University and a B.A. (mathematics) from the University of Iowa. In addition, he has held positions in consulting firms in the private sector and has consulted with state and federal governmental agencies, lawyers, educational systems, and corporations.

In 1980, he and his colleagues pioneered efforts that resulted in developing a videotape-based process to educate statistical consultants in both the technical and the interpersonal aspects of statistical consulting. This process applied quality improvement tools to statisticians themselves to systematically improve the quality of their services. In 1985, he began to apply quality improvement tools to the large lecture introductory business statistics course he was teaching. Again, the intention was to systematically improve the quality of services provided by statisticians. This experience has illustrated the myriad difficulties of applying to one's self what one has preached to others. He has published one book on the human side of statistical consulting and is the author of more than 30 articles on these topics.

Quality Management (QM)
Delivering Continuous Improvement

Education, Quality, and
Quality Improvement

Education: Are we meeting our obligations? Everyone argues about education. A few think it only requires massive infusions of money to make it right; some want to nibble around the edges of change; a few want basic redirection, while others call for dramatic change (e.g., Banathy, 1991; Branson, 1988; Cuban, 1990; Kirst & Meister, 1985; Nelson, 1992; Newmann, 1991; Osborne & Gaebler, 1992; Perelman, 1990; Pipho, 1991; Rasell & Mishel, 1990). Most thoughtful people agree that business as usual is unacceptable. If we don't question many basic assumptions about schools, schooling, and the delivery of instruction, we are probably doing as good a job of education as can be done. We have reached the "upper limit" of investment, where spending more time and money in trying to do better what we already do will be disappointing (Branson, 1988).

Equipped only with the conventional ways of thinking about, funding, and delivering education, today's teachers are doing as well as can be expected. They are, usually, using the methods and materials applied to them when they were learners. The knowledge base of education has changed; the learner characteristics have changed; and society has changed. But education still attempts to be more efficient—do better by working harder and spending more—instead of identifying its basic clients and reorienting its business. It is difficult to define and deliver total quality when you don't have a firm grip on who the customers are and what you should[1] deliver to them.

Principals, administrators, and board members as part of the educational partnership really want good things to happen for students. Educators have received conflicting and single-issue marching orders from legislators while being under constant threat from pressure groups to respond with one quick fix after another. But things aren't getting much better or, at least, they are not getting better quickly enough for us to feel comfortable about our future.

Caring. We care about our schools and our children. In spite of this caring, the cries for better schools continue. New legislation continues to be passed. Most new laws tinker with the resources and means of education (choice, extended school hours and days, fiscal accountability, year-round schooling, tougher courses, full-service schools, merit pay, class size, computer-assisted instruction, school-based management, teacher testing, competency-based certification, and so on).

The more imposed (and quick-fix) initiatives fail (Kirst & Meister, 1985), the more the legislatures attempt to solve educational performance problems by laws and micro management. They tinker with the means before defining useful ends; they don't use strategic thinking or apply the lessons of QM. But, all the while, the rhetoric of "quality" creeps into most conversations.

The more we talk about quality, the less it seems to become a reality. If education is to deliver on its promise to help learners become better citizens for tomorrow, QM is an excellent vehicle for shifting from words to deeds, from rhetoric to accomplishment.

Beyond caring. Caring isn't enough. Changing isn't enough. Spending more money isn't enough. Raising standards is not enough. In fact, each of the single-issue quick fixes imposed upon education might be failing for the wrong reasons. We care about learners and learning, but we don't really know what to deliver and do.

We have never defined "quality" in education, let alone organized to deliver it. It isn't that we don't care about learners. We do. It isn't that we don't realize that our cultural and economic survival depends upon successful learners who become contributing citizens. We do. It isn't that we don't know how to make education more streamlined or don't know how to design educational experiences that will deliver predictable learning. We do. Success can come from thinking about and acting strategically to define and deliver quality, but not simply from throwing more money and people at the schools. We can work much smarter than we have been working.

Until now, we have failed to define and deliver education in the context of quality: providing that which will be useful to those who can use it, where they can use it and when they should have it, and empowering them to use it effectively.

New programs. Educators have not been shy about trying new things in the past. We have seen program after program and hot idea after hot idea piled onto educators. Also, well-meaning legislative mandates are dumped one upon another based on the enduring popular view that our educational system has failed. Putting aside the raging debates on what might be causing the problems, and how best to reverse education's fortunes, educators and citizens alike are searching for ways to help develop successful citizens for tomorrow. Not meeting our challenge is not because of lack of intention or ill will.

As is the case for most human beings and their organizations, change in education doesn't come easily. We know things could and must be better, yet the siren call for business as usual is reinforced by the popular citizen perception that "the nation's schools are awful, but mine is OK." Change we must—but we don't want change for its own sake.

Most educators are no longer satisfied simply to see their learners pass courses or even graduate and get jobs. They also want them to be successful and contributing citizens. Today's professionals want to help create a better world, not just send completers off to the job market. We want to truly provide learning opportunities so that today's learners will become tomorrow's empowered and equipped citizens. These well-prepared future citizens will, in turn, fashion a better world for their children.

Enlightened employers want associates with a spark of excitement about work, the organization, and their mutual contributions—employees who want to be full partners in a quality environment. Tomorrow's employees will have to be up-to-date, competent, confident, and caring people who seek quality continuously. They will actively care about our collective future. We must provide our students—tomorrow's employees and neighbors—with skills, knowledge, attitudes, abilities, and values so they can and will choose to live quality at work and at home.

Many things have been tried that have usually been incomplete or fragmented. Such ideas as team teaching, differentiated staffing, accountability, strategic planning, program evaluation review technique (PERT), open schools, and student choice have been used. While most of these initiatives are basically good ideas, they didn't meet their promise. Often, they failed for the wrong reasons. Not that they were wrong, but they didn't have a connection to the total system and thus were isolated (and neutralizable) from the educational mainstream.

Missing components. We suggest that the components that have been missing from efforts to improve education are

1. a shared vision of the kind of world we want (and are willing to create) for tomorrow's child;
2. defined, measurable educational objectives related to an ideal vision; objectives that, when achieved, will delight the learner and our fellow citizens;

3. a "corporate culture" in education where everyone shares a passion to move continuously closer to the ideal vision and accomplishment of the objectives;

4. a view of education as a service to clients, including learners, parents, and community (this view holds that learners are *not* a product but full participants in the processes and results);

5. a process, or vehicle, that fosters and encourages success in schools for learners, their parents, and all citizens; and

6. a record-keeping system in which our progress is tracked and what's working and what isn't are identified so education can continuously be improved.

Quality management. Although in the molding for more than 50 years, an important process—a way of thinking and acting—has recently caught the attention of concerned educators. The process is called *quality management*[2] or *QM*. QM is a solid process both conceptually and practically. It provides the "glue" for substantial and continuous educational improvement. It incorporates several of the just-noted missing components.

Pioneered by Shewhart (1931), Deming (1986), Juran (1979), and Feigenbaum (1951) in the United States before and during World War II, QM was not accepted by U.S. companies after the war was over. Rather, Japanese industrialists embraced it, inspired by courses taught by Deming and Juran in the early 1950s, and changed their corporate culture to adopt Deming's principals. Unlike conventional quality control methods, Deming's approach put the client in center focus and suggested that everything should be devoted to customer satisfaction.

So sensible is QM, it is tempting to dismiss it as something we do already. We don't. So basic is QM, it is tempting to reject it as demanding impossible changes to an already successful operation. Excuses are seductive alternatives to making QM a part of daily life, a change that has been proven worthy in every respect. QM is rational and practical. Others are pulling it off—as seen in the delight of their clients and the success of the organizations who put it to work.

Quality management—continuous improvement, client satisfaction, positive return on investment, doing it right the first time and every time—should be the intentions of any organization that resolves to make a contribution. Educators, like their counterparts in the private and public sectors, are getting serious about success. Viewing the contributions of quality improvement initiatives worldwide, educational leaders, from the classroom to the board room, are finding the will and the ways to define and create quality.

Our approach agrees with and then builds upon the conventional quality management (QM) process. We provide an additional level of consideration: the success and well-being of tomorrow's child in tomorrow's world. We call this added dimension *quality management plus* (QM+). Let's first address QM and later in the book we will provide the "plus."

Quality Management

Intending to do it right the first time, and every time, and improve constantly, as you learn. If you are not constantly improving, you are falling behind. The world is changing, and our survival depends upon remaining responsive while being responsible. As one advertiser noted, "If it ain't broke, fix it." Deming (1986) was right all along, and we are now starting to realize that his guidance for defining and achieving quality is not just for others but is right for us—today and tomorrow.

Just-in-time concern for quality—for both business and education. The pilgrimage to achieve "total quality"—delivering what the client wants, can use, and should have—is prudent, imperative, and timely. Our national accomplishments are revealing growing deficits, which if not reversed could have drastic consequences. A note of hope is that those who implement QM correctly, with the proper commitment and consistent follow-through, show impressive—if not immediate—results (U.S. General Accounting Office, 1991).

Many people in a wide variety of organizations are applying Deming's concepts, which we once discounted and thought didn't fit "the way we do things in the United States." Total quality management[3] (TQM) is popping up everywhere. Both public and private sector organizations are deeply committed to quality initiatives—thrusts to "do it right the first time and every time."

Based on the Japanese industrial successes and their domination of many world markets, there are increasingly penetrating pleas for education to help make the United States once again competitive. While businesses are responding by pursuing quality management, attention is now turning to do likewise in and for our schools. This thrust may be just in time to help create the kind of future we want for tomorrow's child.

Not only do organizations who want to survive realize that they have to define and achieve total quality, there must be continuous improvement in what organizations use, do, produce, and deliver. Some are doing quality management and continuous improvement well. Others, however, are missing crucial aspects and commitments or overemphasize one dimension to the detriment of others. What follows is how to improve the quality and usefulness of education—continuously.

Basic Elements of Quality Management (QM)

Total quality management and continuous improvement—we will call the integrated process of defining and achieving total quality on a continuous improvement basis *quality management* (QM)—intend to deliver to clients what they want and should have when they want and should have it. When QM is successful, the client will be satisfied—delighted, in fact—with what is delivered. Quality may be defined as providing what is required as judged by the client.

Organizations that have successfully pursued QM have done four things: (a) They have focused organizational attention on meeting client requirements; (b) senior management led the way—modeled—the building of quality values into all operations; (c) all associates were properly trained, developed, and empowered to continuously improve themselves as well as what they did and delivered; and (d) everyone used a systematic and systemic process for continued improvement (U.S. General Accounting Office, 1991). With QM, there is discipline and disciplined caring.

It doesn't seem to matter if the organization is large or small or what its business is. Substantive improvement of performance takes an average of 2-3 years, so successful leaders allow for systematic evolution rather than being tempted to press for short-term, quick gains. The entire system must be involved, not just one area or operation.

Deming's 14 Points and Profound Knowledge:
Putting Them to Work

Deming defines 14 characteristics of a quality management approach[4] (Galagan, 1991; Joiner, 1985):

1. Create constancy of purpose.
2. Adopt a new philosophy.
3. Cease dependence on mass inspection to achieve quality.
4. End the practice of awarding business on price alone. Instead, minimize total cost, which is often accomplished by working with a single supplier.
5. Improve constantly the system of production and service.
6. Institute training on the job.
7. Institute leadership.
8. Drive out fear.
9. Break down barriers between departments.
10. Eliminate slogans, exhortations, and numerical targets.
11. Eliminate work standards (quotas) and management by objective.
12. Remove barriers that rob workers, engineers, and managers of their right to pride of workmanship.
13. Institute a vigorous program of education and self-improvement.
14. Put everyone in the company to work to accomplish the transformation.

These steps represent a major departure from how conventional organizations do business—so different that the introduction of

Deming's steps met initial resistance and often derision. QM works primarily because it is rational. Involving everyone in defining and delivering quality is so sensible, one has to wonder what took everyone, even Deming, so long to "discover" and adopt it.

In addition to the 14 points, Deming (1990) speaks of a system of "profound knowledge" as being an essential part of quality improvement. This system includes (a) appreciation for a system and some knowledge of (b) the theory of variation, (c) the theory of knowledge, and (d) psychology. Organizations must not only change how they do business, they also have to reinvent the organization if they expect to exist in the next century. Sensing the urgency, education, finally, is climbing aboard the quality management train.

The three clusters of Deming's 14 points: Joiner's triangle. Joiner (1985, 1986) groups Deming's 14 points into three clusters:

- a passion for quality,[5]
- scientific approach (data-based decision making), and
- "all on one team."

Joiner's triangle, as we have modified it, is shown in Figure 1.1. Joiner's three clusters of Deming's 14 points provide a road map for the production of systematic quality improvement.

Putting the quality concepts to work: Zahn's triangles. Building on Joiner's triangle, Zahn adds two additional triangles, as shown in Figure 1.2. To make useful data-based decisions, one must systematically generate knowledge. To do this requires that the quality team use statistics, accountability, and interpersonal relationships effectively.

Statistical tools[6] and concepts are essential to the generation of knowledge. For these tools to be effectively used, all persons on the team must be willing to hold themselves accountable (delivering what they said they would deliver) for their part of the process being studied. They must be willing to have data gathered that will assess how well they are accomplishing the tasks for which they are accountable. Accountability and results are never used for blaming but

Figure 1.1. Modified Version of Joiner's Triangle Summarizing Deming's 14 Points
SOURCE: Based in part on Joiner (1986).

only for continuously improving. To know what to keep and what to fix, good data are vital.

Empowering relationships among the quality team members are essential. Dealing effectively with statistics and accountability is not enough. Because all quality improvement occurs when working with others—in a quality improvement team—the usefulness of the problem-solving process of the team is no greater than the quality of the relationships among those engaged in that process. For example, if trust is lacking in the relationships, information may be withheld by one party that might compromise the usefulness of the problem-solving process—and everyone would lose.

Therefore we have found it useful to identify the characteristics of empowering relationships. When there is no alignment on purposes, then relationships may become adversarial. And adversarial relationships rarely lead to high quality results. When there is alignment on purposes, then the relationship is cooperative.

If, in addition, the parties promise to be honest with each other and to "clean up" any results of any dishonesty as soon as they become aware of it, the relationship is one that we call a "working relationship." It will reliably produce the results that the parties intend.

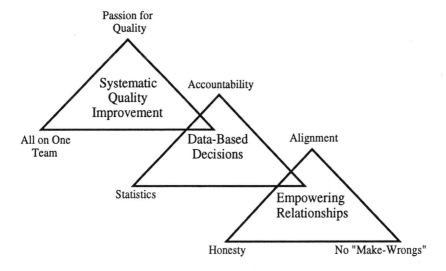

Figure 1.2. Zahn's Triangles, Which Expand on Deming's 14 Points and Joiner's Summary

An even more effective relationship, which we call an "empowering relationship," occurs when both parties give up the right to overtly or covertly belittle, put down, or ridicule ("make-wrong") the other and promise to clean up any "make-wrongs" as soon as they surface.

What a Quality Team Does and Delivers

By clustering elements in the ways Joiner and Zahn suggest, it becomes clear that (a) everyone in the organization has to define and continuously pursue quality, every minute of every day, with every act and decision moving toward its achievement; (b) quality flows from constantly improving the processes, not relying on inspection; and (c) a team spirit—a corporate culture—where everyone contributes, individually and together, will achieve quality for the customer. Let's see what these three steps provide:

1. The quality of what gets delivered outside the organization is more important than anything else—no excuses.

2. Inspection is not effective for delivering quality, for about 85% of all problems are system difficulties and less than 15% are due to workers: the 85/15 rule of Deming and the 80/20 rule of Juran (Joiner, 1986; Oberle, 1990). Thus fixing the processes—making the product right the first time and every time—is essential to delivering quality. You cannot "inspect quality into a product." Blaming workers—including students and teachers—just misses the point on how to deliver quality.

3. Decisions on what to keep and what to change must be made on the basis of valid data and analysis of results and within the context of empowering relationships. Decisions are not to be made on the basis of bias, intuition, or power but on scientific decision making using sensible and sensitive statistical performance data. We realize that performance is variable. As we pursue quality, we aim to reduce—ideally to zero—the variability.

4. Everyone must be headed toward the same set of results; all must be on one team. If everyone is not committed to a common definition of quality—a shared destination—then what gets produced and delivered will surely suffer.

The basic components involved in a QM process. Let's take a brief look at the ingredients of QM in the private sector—proven to be so successful—and note the lessons to be learned for any educational enterprise. Figure 1.3 identifies the basic components of QM, which start with quality ingredients, and applies correct factors of production, which turn out products that, when delivered to clients, earn their satisfaction.

The basic components of a conventional educational (total) quality management process are provided in Figure 1.4.

Assuring that the resources, methods, products, and deliverables are of uniform and consistent high quality—QM—makes sense.[7] Without QM, most organizations don't have much of a future.

Figure 1.3. The Linked Elements in a Conventional (Total) Quality Management Project

Although Deming supplies a conceptual framework, the continuous task of translating his steps and guidance into action remains. What follows will move you from the concepts to designing, installing, implementing, and institutionalizing a quality team, and a quality system, to achieve quality results and payoffs.

Balance. All three QM clusters—a passion for quality, client satisfaction through a shared commitment to delivering quality, and the use of data-based decision making—must be both present and in balance. Successful QM processes avoid emphasizing one cluster over the others. For example, a singular emphasis upon scientific data collection and data-based decision making that simply involves collecting and providing quality control data, using sophisticated data collection methods, or generating reams of diagrams and charts won't deliver total quality. Setting up extensive workshops and seminars about total quality without combining them with data-based decisioning and with shared intention to deliver client satisfaction won't be successful. Nor will continuous cheerleading, slogans, posters, and motivational/hype meetings deliver total quality.

Figure 1.4. The Linked Elements in a Conventional (Total) Quality Management Project for Education

The three clusters of QM, based on Deming's 14 points, must be balanced and applied together. Quality *is* free (Crosby, 1979), but it must be developed, nurtured, and supported with all parts in harmony. Quality must be achieved through everyone being on one team to deliver quality using performance data to decide how best to succeed and please the client.

QM Is a "People" Process

Quality management is a process. It is never complete. Quality and client satisfaction constitute the continuing QM goal. Total quality management is a continuous process by which all of the factors of production, including the most valuable one of all—people—"do it right, the first time and every time."

QM operates as if each person in the organization were the actual customer: making things as if they were going to buy and use them themselves. If we are building cars, we want them to be functional, comfortable, economical, and reliable. When we are in the education business, we constantly work to make certain that every learner will be successful. When we are in the health care business, we want every patient to be correctly diagnosed, helped, and properly treated—

no exceptions. People—caring, concerned, and motivated—make the difference between organizational success and failure.

QM intends to create an organizational climate that encourages continuous improvement toward perfection. It encourages all employees to buy in to the process. QM does not force adherence or compliance but provides each employee with the opportunity to become a full partner in defining and creating success; it invites everyone to achieve, day by day, minute by minute, total quality and total client satisfaction. Everyone is supported, aided, encouraged, and empowered to make a unique contribution to the total quality effort. The more the commitment to total quality is systemwide, the better it will be achieved.

Quality cannot be delegated. All the top people must serve as role models and sponsors for quality. It is better to continue business as usual than it is to "fake" quality management by having the top person "looking down" on the quality process and not being a fully committed player. Systemwide commitment and action are vital if an organization is to define and deliver quality.

Table 1.1 presents several distinctions between two approaches to education: conventional and QM. The QM approach emphasizes serving the learners and continuously improving the system.

Enrolling partners in making quality happen. QM is so important that many organizations are training their associates to be able to "do it right, the first time and every time." For QM to work, everyone—from chief executive officer to janitor, from teacher to board chairperson, from the principal to the teacher's aide—must hold the same vision: total quality to the customer. Good intentions, slogans, and glittering generalities are not enough to deliver success. We have to be specific: Define quality objectives, develop criteria for measuring accomplishments, and identify what has to be done to get us from where we are to our success "vision."

Quality management doesn't stop with an award or even a happy customer. It requires that quality improvement and client satisfaction be continuous. This year's excellent organization can be next year's "also-ran."

QM is not for everyone—at least at first. If any associate doesn't see the benefits of it and what it might deliver, then encourage him

Table 1.1 Foci of Two Approaches to Education: Conventional and QM

Conventional	QM
Conformance to specifications	*Client satisfaction and success*
Control learner	*Self-control*
System defines quality	*Clients define quality*
Learner is passive	*Learner is active*
Frequent inspection	*Continuous improvement*
Cost driven	*Results driven*
Budget-driven plans	*Plan-driven budgets*
If it works don't change	*If it works change*
Quality in after-the-fact	*Quality is continuous and starts with plans*
Change is expensive	*Change is profitable*
Education costs	*Education pays*

or her to opt out. If QM is not part of the corporate culture, shared by all, then everyone is better off allowing those who don't enroll to go their own way. (In fact, they might be assisted, in a nonpunitive manner, to find career opportunities where their values are compatible with that of the majority.)

What Is the "Q" in QM?

Usually, client satisfaction, or dissatisfaction, is based on the perceived quality of the outputs. If most customers believe their Cadillac is the finest auto they have ever owned, then that Division gets about one third of the total points for winning a Malcolm Baldrige Award. If the clients like the parcel delivery system, they give it repeat business and tell their associates. Output quality and customer satisfaction are the vision targets for QM. And satisfaction comes from everyone in the organization, from sweeper to president, working constantly to achieve customer satisfaction.

QM emphasizes that it is important for all elements to fit together. They should mesh to smoothly turn raw materials, through competent and caring processes, into the products and deliverables that satisfy clients. QM enrolls everyone in the partnership for quality—suppliers and workers, sellers and buyers—in defining and achieving the vision: delivering total quality.

Quality in education involves animate, dynamic, changing, and changeable inputs—learners, teachers, administrators. The service aspects of total quality in education must account for the differences between dealing with hardware and being responsive and responsible to live humans (Lawton, 1991).

Quality depends upon a common passion for excellence, with everyone contributing to a common effort. Quality also depends upon accurate and complete performance data: a quality system for collecting and providing scientific data for making quality decisions. A quality system will track results of contributions at each organizational elements level. The details of this important quality system are the topic of Chapter 5.

The QM process: Rolling up to achieve client satisfaction. Figure 1.5 shows the elements of the typical QM process. It starts with the best ingredients and then turns those into products and outputs that meet customer expectations.

Assuring that QM is responsive and responsible. A litmus test of total quality is how well we deliver useful educational products and outputs as the learners go through school and enter our shared society. Another critical test is how well the outputs serve the clients who receive the learners and pay the bills for education.

QM, like the course of true love, doesn't always run smooth. As we continuously improve our quality—that is, ask and answer the basic questions of education (we will discuss these in the next

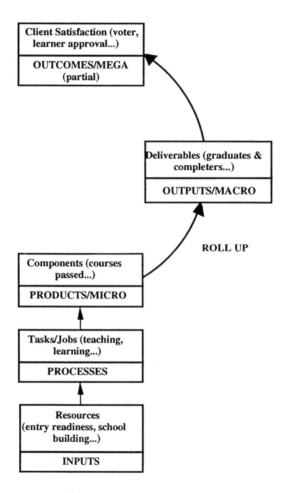

Figure 1.5. A Typical (Total) Quality Management Process
SOURCE: Kaufman (1992b).
NOTE: The quality inputs roll up to processes and then produce products.
These roll up to outputs that are delivered to please clients.

chapter, as presented in Table 2.3)—our path will not be uniform or steady. Nothing is perfect, although we strive to be perfect. We will have variability in our progress and accomplishments. We will learn from our mistakes and apply lessons learned continuously to achieve total quality. We must avoid biasing our quest by asking incomplete or inappropriate questions of ourselves, our partners, and our educational system. QM includes asking, answering, and delivering on the right questions—Table 2.3—using appropriate criteria.

A Commitment to Achieve a Better Future

One of the things we haven't systemically done in education is to commit every person involved in and with education to defining and achieving quality. We have talked about quality in the past, but now there are some concepts and practices that will deliver it. When we commit to total quality, we get a positive return on our investment; quality pays, it doesn't just cost.

A commitment to quality in education requires continuous, active contributions to the improvement of what we use, do, and deliver. It is more than a project here and a program there. QM is a transformation.

No one-shot efforts will suffice. Quality becomes a way of life. We are what we do, and, when we "do quality," everyone wins.

Everyone in education is focused on the learners and preparing them to be successful individuals and contributing neighbors. What we do and deliver must be designed to help learners help themselves to be successful. We learn both from what works and from what doesn't. We don't blame anyone when we fail to meet our objectives, we revise and continuously improve.

QM is a caring way of doing things. When we use it, we care so much for everyone in the system that we apply science to our continuous improvement. No more acting on the basis of biases, opinions, hunches, and power plays. Learners and their success are far too important to trust to our instincts and hunches. Decisions are to be based on performance data. We will collect data on our accomplishments and compare them with our intentions.

We know that performance—students in schools as well as the fabrication of electronic components on an assembly line—is variable (we often use statistical tools such as standard deviation, standard error, dispersion, and variance to measure this variability), and we realize that progress will often have ups and downs as we move toward our objectives. Instead of being disturbed by variability, we learn from it and make changes to assure we are making progress toward our objectives.

*   *   *

What follows in this book is a look at how an educational agency can get a QM effort defined and running. Chapter 2 provides the basics. Chapter 3 describes a strategy for implementing QM in your school or district.

Notes

1. When we use the word *should*, we are not intending to be prescriptive and arbitrary. We realize that, all too often, people attempt to wrest power from others for themselves by telling them what they "should" do or even what they "need." Rather, we use *should* from the perspective of moving to bring about a better shared tomorrow for ourselves, our children, and our society—as best as we can ascertain it. We will use *must* in the same way.

2. Terms and labels abound: *total quality management* (TQM), *continuous improvement* (CI), and *quality management* (QM). Each has its champions and detractors. We will, while dignifying the usefulness of each term, move continuously toward using *quality management*. Included in QM is the concept of continuous improvement. Thus each time we use QM, please mentally include CI and the intention to move to achieve total success as an integral part of that concept and the process.

3. Deming doesn't seem to care for the *total quality management* label, but the term endures anyway. The "big three" of quality— Deming, Juran, and Crosby—seem to share more considerations in common than differences (Oberle, 1990). But differences do exist that seem more important to advanced TQM researchers and programs than to those in the early inception stages. We prefer the term *quality management*.

4. As you review them, remember that they are intended for private sector organizations. These concepts will be tailored to education in Chapter 2.

5. This is actually a modification of one of Joiner's elements. Rather than using *obsession*, we substitute *passion*.

6. Many people, unfortunately, freeze when even the term *statistics* is introduced. It doesn't have to be a worry. Statistics are basically sensible, understandable, and straightforward. In Chapter 5, we will prove that.

7. The QM process is rational, especially when it goes beyond simple "ticket-punching" and compliance with arbitrary process-oriented award guidelines. There is growing concern in the private sector that some organizations are missing the point of QM and are simply jumping hurdles to get an award. QM should be part of the organizational culture only because it is the right thing to do—for everyone.

Elements of QM
in Education

Is QM Appropriate
for Education?

QM and education. QM, when properly and consistently applied, benefits all types of organizations. Education, and all of its partners, also can benefit from QM. All organizations, public and private, have many similar features that are amenable to quality processes.

As do other organizations, we in education have external clients: the citizens who hire our outputs as well as pay the taxes. Education also must demonstrate results—*products*, including learners who complete courses and graduate (or get licenses in a vocational area). In addition, we have *processes*, those factors of production (we call them *teaching, learning, activities, curriculum,* and so on) that deliver results. And, finally, we have *inputs*, or ingredients: existing resources, buildings, teachers, and the skills, knowledge, attitudes, and abilities the learners bring to our schools.

QM in education links these elements, assuring that they all fit together smoothly and that all parties, including the learners, become active participants in achieving quality. In education, as elsewhere, quality is assessed by examining the results we deliver: Quality learners are competent, confident, and can perform on the job. Quality educational *outputs* (graduates and completers) not only get jobs but make a contribution to their organization's clients. In other words, they have the attitudes and abilities to participate in quality initiatives where they work.

No doubt, education, as does any other organization, uses resources, develops products, and delivers outputs to external clients. It links ends and means to help learners become competent in today's and tomorrow's worlds. Although we usually use more tender words for our educational concerns and activities than does business, we deliver an output that is paid for, and judged by, society.

The truth is that we can do better in education. We can, and must, get much better results. Doing so may be just as simple as deciding to put quality in the forefront of all of our planning, development, and delivery. Perhaps what's been missing has been the commitment to define and deliver quality—on purpose and continuously.

The Building Blocks of QM:
What's Involved

Changing the Way We View the World:
Shifting Our Paradigms and Our Mental Gears

The world, its people, and their values and demands don't stand still—even for education. If education is defaulting on its promissory note to its learners and citizen partners, why would it simply continue to do what it is now doing, just more efficiently? Breaking out of decades-long habits requires a major shift in how we think and transact with our world if we are to take the simple and not always easy step of committing to QM.[1]

Thomas Kuhn (1962, 1970) told us about paradigm shifts—moving from one set of assumed boundaries and operating rules to another.[2] The evidence of lost opportunities because we refused to accept that there has been a paradigm shift is all around us. Some examples are the Swiss rejecting digital watches (their own invention) and losing most of the world market; the United States not believing it important to make better designed and more fuel efficient cars and giving overseas manufacturers a huge hunk of our former business. We have to prevent the same misfortunes for education.

The world has changed on us and will continue to do so. If we persist in applying old paradigms—boundaries and outmoded rules—to new realities, we will continue to fall behind and increasingly have to race to keep up. Ultimately, we will drop from exhaustion. In education, we seem to be experiencing the same kind of drain and collapse. With high hopes, and with continued sizable increases in spending for the resources and methods for delivering education, it is now obvious that these arcane responses don't deal with the new realities, parameters, and paradigms. The new educational paradigm is one of contributing to societally useful results, not simply teaching subjects to learners and hoping for the best.

Instead of relying on tired and self-defeating techniques and mind-sets, instead of using outmoded guidelines and decision rules, we can benefit from being proactive and holistic. We can search for, and understand, new visions, relationships, and paradigms. When we open ourselves and do this, we allow new directions, boundaries, and rules.

We can stop being self-limiting and open ourselves to new directions and new opportunities based on new realities. Seeing that most conventional approaches don't deliver the results we must have, there is higher risk in continuing what we are now doing than in shifting to new boundaries—parameters—and new rules for thinking, planning, and doing (Banathy, 1991; Branson, 1988; Drucker, 1992; Kaufman, 1992a, 1992b; Osborne & Gaebler, 1992).

Being open and enterprising is so important that it is the first of six critical success factors for continuous improvement of educational quality. Before we go into the details, preview all of the success factors, which are shown in Table 2.1, but realize that we will fully explain each as we progress.

Table 2.1 The Six Critical Success Factors (CSF) for QM

Critical Success Factor 1:	Be willing to move out of today's comfort zones and use new and wider boundaries for thinking, planning, doing, and evaluating.
Critical Success Factor 2:	Use and link all three levels of results (mega, macro, and micro) for defining and delivering quality.
Critical Success Factor 3:	Everyone demonstrates a passion for quality: Everything everyone does, constantly and consistently, is directed toward improving the quality of what is used, done, and delivered.
Critical Success Factor 4:	Everyone—learners, teachers, administrators, parents, employers, neighbors—is on the same team. Quality is what everyone is after, and everyone will make a unique and collective contribution to achieve it.
Critical Success Factor 5:	All decisions are made on the basis of solid, objective, relevant performance data.
Critical Success Factor 6:	Building a cooperative team—whose members learn from each other and put the purposes of the QM+ effort above comfort and continuously improve—is the key for moving from quality intention to realization.

Six critical success factors. Critical success factors—CSFs—are those actions that must be taken to successfully implement QM (Kaufman, 1992b, 1992c, 1992d).

Now, let's get back to some of the details of the very important and overriding Critical Success Factor 1. *Do we really have to change our ways?* Yes! *Do we really have to move from our current paradigms— understandings and assumptions—of how education works?* Yes! If we aren't the masters of change, we will surely be the victims of it. If we only curse today's problems and solutions, we will not be open to creating a new quality education and a new reality. CSF 1 is important for defining and delivering total quality.

CSF 1 is for all those people who don't believe that current educational results are satisfactory, that we are not delivering quality in education. It is for all of those who realize that today's and tomorrow's worlds are different than those upon which most educational curriculum and delivery are based. No longer are we (if we ever were) in the era of *Ozzie & Harriet, The Brady Bunch,* and *Happy*

Days, where the norm was nuclear families, the air seemed to be clean, and life was simply a matter of the kids worrying about their dates for Saturday night.

Shifting How We View and Interact With Our World: Overcoming Myopia

From splintering to holistic system thinking. We have learned and been rewarded for some bad habits. U.S. organizations have been successful, but in a perhaps more pliable world. The world is now less forgiving. We now know we just can't work harder, faster, longer. We have to shift from a reactive (fixing current crises) to a proactive mode—creating a new reality. We have believed that, by reducing everything to its smallest piece, we can find understanding of the whole. We have lived and survived in a world where we fragment, splinter, analyze, and develop. We view things through a magnifying glass that exaggerates everything under view and encourages us to ignore the larger context (Kaufman, 1992e), even though system thinking—relating the whole and the parts—has been available for several decades; for example, see Ackoff and Sasieni (1968), Buckley (1968), Carter (1969), Checkland (1981), Kaufman (1972), Morgan and Chadwick (1971), Senge (1990), and Von Bertalanffy (1968).

We tend to teach subjects and not learners. We accept without question that the sum total of conventional courses (math, science, music, and so on) will provide learners with what they have to know and be able to do for current and future survival, self-sufficiency, and well-being. Figure 2.1 shows the conventional subject-based planning tactics. But what about the "blank spaces"[3] (total requirements for future functioning) not covered by conventional content areas? How will learners master what is not available in the curriculum?

We splinter our curriculum and content and thus miss both the coverage of vital areas as well as the synergies among topics and areas.

The Three Levels of Educational Results: Mega, Macro, and Micro

QM involves the total system—the entire organization. While it is tempting to restrict a QM process to one part of an organization

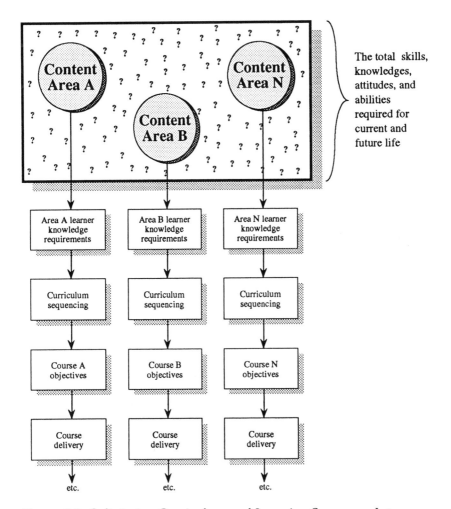

Figure 2.1. Splintering Curriculum and Learning Sequences Into Disciplines, or Content Areas, Doesn't Include the "Blank Spaces" of What Education Should Deliver

(manufacturing, elementary school, physics course, counseling, central office), the total organization—everyone and everything—is involved in defining and achieving success. Let's look at the entire organization, identify its elements, and see how each organizational element must be included and interrelated in QM.

Three levels of organizational results and contributions. Often over-looked in educational thinking, planning, and evaluation is the fact that there are three levels of results. The most basic level—see Question 1 in Table 2.2—has a mega focus. It is concerned with societal and community outcomes and consequences. An example of a mega-level result is that all learners will be self-sufficient and not be under the care, custody, or control of another person, agency, or substance.

The most usual focus of educational missions is at the macro (see Question 2) level, such as "at least 90% of all learners will graduate." At the macro level, the agency or school level is the primary client and beneficiary of any contributions, or outputs, of the organization.

Still a third is the micro level: being concerned with individual products or small group accomplishments (Question 3), such as improved course completion in math and science or pass rate at the college admission level for the SAT.

All of these questions, whether formally recognized or not, haunt every organization. If we choose not to answer—and link—all three, we face an ethical quandary: If education is the solution, what's the problem? If we do not intend for all learners to be successful, self-sufficient, self-reliant, socially responsive, and responsible citizens, then what do we have in mind? If we are not a means to useful societal ends, what basis do we have for existing?

These three levels of results are "nested": Mega results are built up from macro-level ones, which in turn are an integration and collection of micro-level results.

Consideration of all three levels of results is essential for success using QM, as is emphasized by Critical Success Factor 2 (CSF 2) for continuous improvement:

Critical Success Factor 2: **Use and link all three levels of results (mega, macro, and micro) for defining and delivering quality.**

There is great power in aligning everything we use, do, and deliver with the long-term mega-level vision, mission, and building-block results. After all, if we don't intend to make a positive contribution to today's and tomorrow's worlds, what *do* we have in mind?

Table 2.2 Three Basic Strategic Planning Questions and the Type of Planning Associated With Each as Well as Who Is the Primary Client and Beneficiary of Each

Strategic Questions	Type of Planning	Primary Client and Beneficiary
1. Are we concerned with the current and future self-sufficiency, self-reliance, and quality of life of the world in which we and our learners live?	MEGA	Society
2. Are we concerned with the quality of life that our organization delivers to society?	MACRO	Educational System or School
3. Are we concerned with the quality of that which is turned out within our system and is used by internal clients as they do the business of the educational system?	MICRO	Individual or Small Group

SOURCE: Based on Kaufman (1992a, 1992b).

Two levels of educational methods and resources. While we educators spend most of our time and effort in doing things—delivering learning opportunities—we often start our thinking and planning at the how-to or resources level and race into action before confirming where we are headed. Activities and resources are important, and we must link these sensibly to our objectives.

Realizing that any organization has basic elements that define what it delivers—three levels of results, plus activities and resources to produce them—allows us to add questions to any organization's menu of what it may be concerned with.

Table 2.3 provides the full array of questions each organization, public and private, may choose to ask and answer. Questions 4 (processes, methods, activities, techniques) and 5 (resources such as teacher competencies, available technology, buildings, equipment) are concerned with the operations of any educational agency. Questions 1-3 deal with ends; 4 and 5 deal with means; and 6 and 7 attend to evaluation.

All levels of planning and doing are vital to quality in education. All the questions shown in Table 2.3 are vital if we are to define and deliver quality in education. Ask yourself and your educational partners the following questions:

1. Which of these questions can we afford to assume answers to or ignore?
2. Which of the questions do we now formally attend to?
3. Which of the questions do we formally link to assure a vertical integration among them?
4. Which of the questions have we committed to both ask and answer?

The Organizational Elements Model (OEM)

A detailed framework for relating what organizations use, do, deliver, and accomplish. Every organization shares some similarities with all others. Each uses ingredients that it forms and shapes into something tangible—products—which include goods and/or services. Then, organizations combine these "tangibles" into something it can deliver to external clients. Finally, the success of the organization depends upon client satisfaction and the usefulness of what was delivered.

Specific labels for these elements allow us to differentiate among them and relate them. Table 2.4 shows the organizational elements, examples of each, and how they define what organizations use, do, and deliver.

QM involves all of the elements in Table 2.4, which are meshed and melded to deliver client satisfaction. A typical QM process

Table 2.3 Organizational Questions All Educators Must Ask and Answer

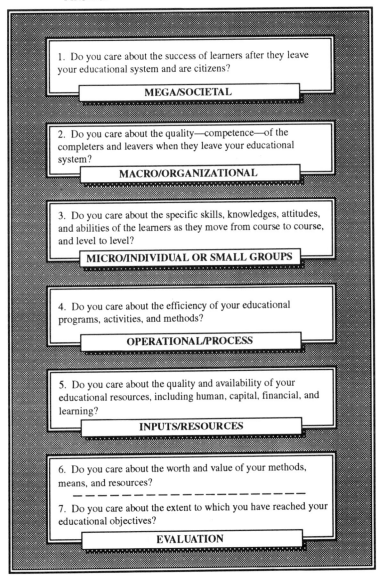

1. Do you care about the success of learners after they leave your educational system and are citizens?

MEGA/SOCIETAL

2. Do you care about the quality—competence—of the completers and leavers when they leave your educational system?

MACRO/ORGANIZATIONAL

3. Do you care about the specific skills, knowledges, attitudes, and abilities of the learners as they move from course to course, and level to level?

MICRO/INDIVIDUAL OR SMALL GROUPS

4. Do you care about the efficiency of your educational programs, activities, and methods?

OPERATIONAL/PROCESS

5. Do you care about the quality and availability of your educational resources, including human, capital, financial, and learning?

INPUTS/RESOURCES

6. Do you care about the worth and value of your methods, means, and resources?

7. Do you care about the extent to which you have reached your educational objectives?

EVALUATION

SOURCE: Kaufman (1992b).
NOTE: Questions 1-3 deal with results; the balance deal with processes, resources, and evaluation.

Table 2.4 The Organizational Elements Model (OEM) and Examples of Each

ORGANIZATIONAL LEVEL	INPUTS (resources, ingredients)	PROCESSES (how-to's; means; methods; procedures)	PRODUCTS (en route –building-block– results)	OUTPUTS (the aggregated products of the system that are delivered or deliverable to society)	OUTCOMES (the contributions of outputs in and for society and the community)
EXAMPLES	Existing personnel; identified needs, goals, objectives, policies, regulations, laws, money, values, and societal and community characteristics; current quality of life, learner entry characteristics, teacher competencies, buildings, equipment, etc.	Quality management - continuous improvement; teaching; learning; in-service training, managing, accelerated learning; site-based managing; accountability; etc.	Course completed; competency test passed; skill acquired; learner accomplishments; instructor accomplishments; etc.	Graduates; completers; dropouts; job placements; certified licensees; etc.	Self-sufficient, self reliant, productive individual who is socially competent and effective, contributing to self and others; no addiction to others or to substances; financially independent; continued funding of agency; etc.
CLUSTER	EFFORTS		RESULTS		SOCIETAL RESULTS/IMPACT
SCOPE	INTERNAL (Organizational)				EXTERNAL (Societal)
PLANNING LEVEL			MICRO	MACRO	MEGA
PRIMARY CLIENT OR BENEFICIARY			INDIVIDUAL OR SMALL GROUP	SCHOOL SYSTEM OR SCHOOL	SOCIETY/COMMUNITY
STRATEGIC QUESTION			Are we concerned with the quality of what is turned out within our system and is used by internal clients as they do the business of the educational system?	Are we to be concerned with the quality of life which our organization delivers to society?	Are we to be concerned with the current and future self-sufficiency, self reliance, and quality of life of the world in which we and our learners live?

SOURCE: Based on Kaufman (1988a).

includes five elements. Three of the elements relate to results (outcomes, outputs, products), one relates to methods (processes), and the other to resources (inputs):

- *Inputs:* raw materials, existing facilities, and available resources; human capital; buildings, equipment; existing objectives, policies, procedures; and finances

In education, inputs include learners, teachers, schools, classrooms, media resources, available learning materials, budgets, board members, preservice training levels and credentials, administrators, parents, community members, lobbyists, legislators, and the historical perceptions of the schools—all of the ingredients an educational system can or must use as it does its work.

Education deals with inputs that are different than the inputs one uses when making widgets. Learners bring with them a rich array of values, abilities, skills, and experiences. It is important that we maintain a humanistic focus that always realizes the human nature of our enterprise.

- *Processes:* production methods and means, activities, applied skills; constructing and fabricating products, robotics, machining, developing; training and human resources development; personnel at work, total quality management initiatives, value engineering

In an educational setting, processes include teaching learners, developing learning materials, scheduling, activities (including athletics, guidance, and cultural endeavors), in-service training of teachers, courses. Processes transform inputs into results. They should add value to the inputs in terms of the results they deliver. Processes are the heart of any educational enterprise. They are where we spend most of our time and commit most of our resources.

Inputs and processes are the factors of production. They supply the ingredients for production and then transform—work with and develop—the raw materials into products.

Products are the micro-level building-block results we get from the transformation of the inputs through application of our process:

- *Products* (micro-level results): fenders, headache tablets, validated training materials, boxes, labels, completed bills, reports, wheels, disk drives, drinking glasses, reading glasses, toasters, a TV

In an educational agency, products include a completed course, an instructional video disk, a filed attendance report, an accomplished counseling objective, a lost football game, an approved strategic plan, a passed literacy exam, a delivered orchestra recital. Products in education are the building blocks of the system. Our curriculum specifies the learning results that must be obtained (often noted in Carnegie Units). The educational products are the individual learner and teacher contributions. We keep score on our products with grades and test results.

But passing a course, or winning a volleyball game, doesn't make an educated individual or assure success in life. Higher-order results now become important: outputs.

Outputs are the macro-level results we can and do deliver to our external clients. Outputs are the integration, the adding-up, of all of the products:

- *Outputs* (macro-level results): an automobile (made up of fenders, chassis, tires, and so on); a prescription drug (including bottle, cotton, pills, label, box); a computer system (including disk drives, keyboard, modem, software, cases, monitor, mouse, instruction books, power cords, printer)

Education, too, has outputs. These include graduates from a high school, an individual who is certified as a licensed vocational nurse, a merit scholar headed for our finest state university, an apprentice mechanic who gets a job with the city bus company. We keep score on our educational outputs; we gather data on graduates, completers, noncompleters, job placements, college entries.

After a learner leaves, completes, graduates, or gets certified, there is an impact: consequences in and for the community and society. These consequences in and for society are termed *outcomes.* Outcomes (as we will detail in Chapter 4) are an important aspect of mega-level results:

- *Outcomes* (mega-level results): repeat customers satisfied with the outputs; a safe automobile; a computer system that helps achieve a profit for the client

Educational outcomes are mega-level results, such as parents satisfied with the quality of education, a learner who gets and keeps a job, a graduate who enters higher education, completes a degree, and gets and keeps a job.

Customer satisfaction—a part (but not all) of mega-level results—must be addressed in typical QM. Satisfaction is determined by the perceived usefulness of the outputs. Do the external clients find them worthy? Will they continue to be customers, or will they demand changes or take their business elsewhere?[4]

Ends and Means: So Simple and So Often Confused

This section and the following one present some basic concepts that will be important as you build a QM partnership in your system. At first, the terms will sound familiar, but, as you give them careful attention, you will realize that these new definitions and uses will be important to all quality partners. We will call on your acceptance of CSF 1, for what follows might bump you up against the limits of your comfort zone.

First, we will speak to ends and means. Next, we will define objectives and needs.

Ends are results, consequences, payoffs. Means are the resources and ways we achieve results. The only rational way to select means is on the basis of the ends to be accomplished. Yet, in education as in all other segments of the society, we assume that our means will deliver useful results. Unfortunately, this is more dream than reality.

The history of modern education revolves around our changing of means (more money, more teachers, less administrators, better credentialing, and so on) in hopes that worthy ends would be delivered. As we noted earlier, hopes are not realities, and means are not ends. To highlight the confusion and the relationship, Table 2.5 shows some ends and means for common educational activities and results. Review them and note how often a means has been selected without defining the end it is to deliver.

Table 2.5 Some Typical Educational Means and Ends

	END	MEANS
Restructuring		X
School-Based Managing		X
Competency-Based Test Item	X	
Total Quality Management		X
Teaching		X
Learning		X
Course Grade	X	
Graduation	X	
Employment	X	
Budget		X
Planning		X
Computer-assisted Instructing		X
Open Enrollments		X
Decentralization		X
Unionization		X
Law		X
Policy		X
Curriculum		X
Classrooms		X
Child Care Program		X
School Lunch Program		X

SOURCE: Kaufman (1992b).

Objectives are ends referenced. If there is one thing that planners and designers agree on, it is that objectives relate to ends, products, accomplishments, results.[5]

Objectives are results focused. They identify

- what is to be accomplished
- who or what will demonstrate the accomplishment[6]
- what criteria will be used to indicate accomplishment
- under what conditions will the accomplishments be observed

All of the above are clearly specified to assure no confusion concerning the results to be delivered.

Another way to characterize an objective is that it states, unmistakably, "where we are going and how we will know when we've arrived." Objectives (sometimes also called *performance standards* or *performance indicators*) provide reliable indicators of accomplishment. Means, on the other hand, are the how-to-do-its, processes, resources, and methods that may be used to achieve results. Means identify the possible ways to achieve desired ends:

Means → Ends

Our language gives us some clues. Almost all English words ending in "ing" are means: plann*ing*, assess*ing*, teach*ing*, work*ing*, learn*ing*, analyz*ing*, tell*ing*, writ*ing*, report*ing*, mak*ing*, buy*ing*, supervis*ing*, manag*ing*.

When preparing objectives, your objectives should focus on ends, not means. After selecting the results to be obtained, then you may sensibly consider and select the best ways to get there. If your intentions are process, or means focused, you will consider alternative methods without explicitly identifying what result you are to get.

For example, select the ends-oriented statements:

1. Improve the efficiency of teaching.
2. Cut the time for mastery of spelling words down by 10 seconds.

Table 2.6 A Format for Preparing Measurable Objectives: As Easy
            as ABCD

A: Who or What is the **A**udience, target, or recipient?

B: What **B**ehavior, performance, accomplishment, end, or re-
        sult is to be demonstrated?

C: Under what **C**onditions will the behavior or accomplishment
        be observed?

D: What **D**ata—criteria, ideally measured on an interval or
        ratio scale—will be used to calibrate success?

SOURCE: Kaufman (1992b).
NOTE: Any objective should include the ABCD elements.

3. Improve supervising methods.

4. Develop computer-based instruction methods.

5. Teach quality management and continuous improvement.

6. Increase graduation rate by at least 11% this year.

7. Assure that my school is a "good neighbor."

Answer: Statements 2, 6, and 7 are the ends-/results-focused
ones.

Any objective should have the same basic elements. One format
includes a mnemonic of ABCD (see Table 2.6).

Table 2.7 provides a simplified example of the application of the
ABCD "rule" to preparing an objective.

Defining Need[7]

We can't overemphasize the importance of how we define this
term. If we use it as a noun—a gap in results, not a deficit in resources
or methods—our quality management process will be unquestion-
ably better. For the purposes of QM, it is vital to use the following
definition:

A *need* is the gap between current results and desired or
required results.

Table 2.7 A Sample Completed ABCD Form

	A Format for Preparing Measurable Objectives: As Easy as ABCD	
	ABCD Element	**Hypothetical Objective**
A:	Who or what is the Audience, target, or recipient?	100% of all learners, completers, and leavers who enrolled at the English-Steffy Unified School District after September 1, 1992.
B:	What Behavior, performance, accomplishment, end, or result is to be demonstrated?	Will be accepted to postsecondary education, and/or get and keep a job that pays at least as much as it costs them to live. None will drop out without meeting state requirements, and all will be self-sufficient.
C:	Under what Conditions will the behavior or accomplishment be observed?	Both in school and beyond exit: Each year, there will be an independent audit of in-school registrations and district records, as well as an independent placement and follow-up study of all completers and leavers.
D:	What Data--criteria, ideally measured on an interval or ratio scale--will be used to calibrate success?	There will be 0 unapproved dropouts, and 0 previously enrolled learners who did not get accepted to a postsecondary program accredited by a regional education commission and/or who did not get and keep a job for at least 6 months (barring seasonal or economic layoffs) as reported and certified by the superintendent.

SOURCE: Kaufman (1992b).

39

A *need* is not a gap in resources, processes, methods, or how-to-do-its (such as money, teacher aides, computers, or televisions). A gap in a method, resource, or process is called a *quasi need*.

Needs are gaps in results, consequences, or accomplishments:[8]

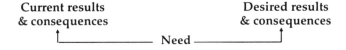

Once the needs are identified, they may be placed in priority order. Based upon the prioritized needs, you then select the best ways and means to get from here to there. Means are the ways—solutions, methods, interventions, programs, activities—to close the gaps to meet the needs:

Current results ———— Means ——→ Desired results
& consequences   & consequences

It's all quite sensible. If there are no gaps between what you deliver (and the consequences) and what you desire to deliver (and those payoffs), you have no needs—you simply keep on doing whatever you are doing. If there are discrepancies, it is time to find a way to close those gaps in results.

If we use *need* as a verb (you "need" to work harder, you "need" to work more hours, and so on), we are prescribing solutions to others; we are taking away their choices and imposing ours. Means should only be selected on the basis of the results we want to accomplish, the needs we wish to reduce or eliminate.

Doing a Needs Assessment
for Quality Management Initiatives

Continuous improvement requires us to continue what's working and change (or drop) what isn't. Doing so requires data, valid and useful data. Recalling that one of Joiner's clusters is data-based decision making, needs assessment data will provide facts—hard data—about our successes and our shortfalls. Let's now turn to what a needs assessment is.

Unlike definitions in educational operations (and conventional wisdom, which is the same conventional wisdom that has gotten us in our current catch-up posture), our definition builds on our emphasis upon ends and objectives being ends focused:

A *needs assessment* identifies gaps between current results and desired (or required) ones, places them in priority order, and selects those to be reduced or eliminated (Kaufman, 1992a, 1992b; Kaufman & Herman, 1991).

Needs assessments

(a) identify gaps between current results and desired ones,

(b) place the needs in priority order, and

(c) select the ones to be addressed.

A needs assessment provides the *needs*—that is, gaps in results— which will allow you to analyze their causes. Only by knowing the needs and their origins can you make rational decisions about what it takes to improve results. The finding of the origins and causes of needs is called *needs analysis* (Kaufman & Valentine, 1989). From the data generated first by a needs assessment and then by a needs analysis (the order is very important), you may identify ways and means to close the gaps.

Any scientific approach requires that decisions be made on the basis of performance data, not upon bias, hunches, or popularly held stereotypes or quick fixes. A useful tool for determining what works and what doesn't is needs assessment. Needs, at least when planning and applying QM, should be defined as gaps between current results and desired ones.

For each element in a quality management process, the gaps in results between "what is" and "what should be" are determined so that useful ways and means for meeting the needs can be selected. For each results-based element in the format suggested in Table 2.8, the needs—gaps between current results (and quality) and desired ones—may be determined. Each element would identify needs as gaps in results at the three levels of mega, macro, and micro.

Table 2.8 A Needs (and quasi-needs: inputs and processes) Assessment Format and Some Examples of Conventional Educational (total) Quality Management Indicators

	Current Results	Current Consequences	Desired Results	Desired Consequences
MEGA LEVEL				
Board Member Satisfaction				
Employer Satisfaction				
Graduate/Completer Success				
Etc...				
MACRO LEVEL				
Number of Graduates				
Vocational Licenses Earned				
Job Placements				
Number Accepted to College				
Etc...				
MICRO LEVEL				
Course Grades				
Absences				
Standardized Test Norms				
Volleyball Win/Loss Record				
Etc...				
(Quasi Needs)				
PROCESS LEVEL				
Computers in use				
Classroom Contact Hours				
Hours of Instruction				
Etc...				
(Quasi Needs)				
INPUT LEVEL				
Quality of Teacher Credentials				
Funding Availability				
Availability of Human Resources				
Facilities				
Equipment				
Clarity of Objectives				
Attitude/Motivation				
Etc...				

SOURCE: Based on Kaufman (1992b).

Needs, Opportunities, and Maintenance

Assuring that needs do not develop, continuing what is successful, and finding opportunities. Not all quality improvement deals with problems or something out of control. We often want to continuously improve what we do and deliver even when there are no current problems. As one advertiser advises, "If it ain't broke, fix it."

Although the definition of *need* is a gap in results, it is very important to keep gaps in results from occurring: to maintain or improve that which is working well. When doing a needs assessment, also identify the areas that should be maintained for which no needs currently exist. Hand in hand with maintenance of what is working is the identification of possibilities and opportunities. Opportunities are results that are not currently obtained or even planned for, such as the development of group problem-solving abilities. Planning and needs assessments deal with

fixing, reactively, that which is not working properly;

assuring that gaps in results in critical areas do not develop; and

identifying what is currently missing and should be designed and developed.[9]

The needs are placed in priority order based upon what it costs, directly and indirectly, to meet the needs versus what it costs to ignore the needs (Kaufman, 1992a). After selecting the needs, it is time to select the best ways and means (including in-service training, mentoring, computer-assisted learning, ungraded schools, local control, vouchers/choice, team-building, and simulation) to achieve quality.

Understanding and applying these concepts—selecting means on the basis of ends; defining needs as gaps in results; using a need assessment approach that identifies needs, prioritizes them, and selects them—are basic to QM. Ends, needs, and needs assessment are basic concepts and tools for providing everyone with valid and useful data for decision making.

*Strategic and Tactical Planning
and Their Relationship to QM*

Strategic planning is a proactive process that identifies the future we want for tomorrow's child and identifies the requirements and means to achieve it (Kaufman, 1992a, 1992b; Kaufman & Herman, 1991). It has a number of steps within four overarching phases: (a) scoping, (b) data collecting, (c) planning, and (d) implementing and evaluating. Figure 2.2 provides a holistic strategic planning framework. QM provides the mind-set, corporate culture, and much of the data to turn an educational strategic plan into educational success. QM provides the glue for the transition from strategic to tactical planning.

Quality management may be the primary vehicle for turning strategic plans to realities. As a process, QM systematically and systemically builds to achieve the shared vision and objectives identified by a strategic plan. In addition, tactical planning identifies the best ways and means to provide the building blocks to achieve the vision and the mission of the educational system or school.

Strategic planning, like its QM partner, may ask and answer important educational questions. The questions that an educational partnership chooses will determine what they intend to accomplish. Table 2.3 provides the menu of educational questions that QM and strategic planning could address.

Your educational partners may select those that they find important to address and answer. After identifying the questions they "care about," then they should commit to delivering on that caring.

Integrating the planning and quality partnerships. By integrating planning and quality, we can, simultaneously, define the right place to head as well as build the team and commitment to get there. Strategic planning best involves the partners who will be responsible for carrying it out. Merge the planning team and the quality team: Everyone will be on one team both to plan and to deliver quality. By having the planners and the quality partners be the same people, we get both buy-in and commitment from their having defined the ideal vision and the mission. Merging the team delivers two critical QM

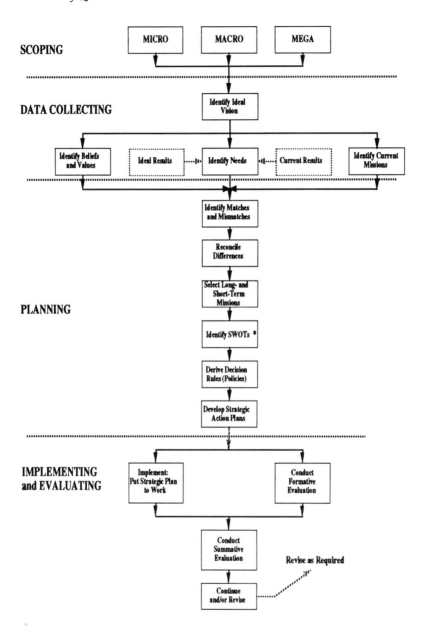

Figure 2.2. A Four-Cluster Strategic Planning Framework: Scoping, Data Collecting, Planning, Implementing, and Evaluating
*Strengths, weaknesses, opportunities, and threats.

ingredients: "all on one team" and a passion for (and measurable definition of) quality.

As the partners do the planning, they will begin the data-based decision-making process—another vital QM element—by (a) collecting needs (gaps in results) data and (b) preparing all objectives (including mission objectives) that target ends and not means. This data-based planning and results-referenced decision making will provide the rational and practical basis for planning what has to be accomplished to get results. Data-based decisioning will also provide the bases for evaluation of progress as the organization continuously improves—moves toward the closer-in objectives and the ideal vision.

Educational organizations often have a number of uncoordinated "improvement" initiatives (usually means/processes) operating at the same time (as we noted above with strategic planning and quality management). Such programs might include those for "accountability," "trust," "coaching," "accelerative learning," "best cost," "team building," and the like. By linking each (and all) of these to an ideal vision and the educational mission objective, integration and synergies may be realized. Many individual improvement initiatives never meet their full potential because they are seen and operated in isolation rather than integrated with a strategic plan and a quality management process.

Selecting the methods and means—tactics and tools—for quality management. Rather than rushing to use old and familiar methods (including ones we notice others employing), we can be creative and select techniques and means on the basis of the costs and benefits they will deliver.

Take the needs—gaps in results—selected and identify possible methods and means for closing them. Don't use any tool, technique, or procedure unless it (a) will close the gaps in results and (b) will do it efficiently. When doing the methods-means analysis, you might consider possible synergies with other organizational activities. Table 2.9 provides a methods-means analysis format.

Evaluating your results and payoffs. Evaluation is finding out what worked and what didn't and seeing which of the objectives were met.

Table 2.9 A Methods-Means Identification Format

| Need* | Current Performer Skills, Knowlege & Abilities | Required Performer Skills, Knowlege & Abilities | Possible Interventions | Cost-Results Analysis | |
				Advantages	Disadvantages

Identify possible ways and means to close the gaps in results

NOTE: Needs may be clustered; several might deal with some common gaps in results.

Based upon the evaluation results, we can tell what to change and what to keep. The criteria for evaluation come directly from the "Desired Results (what should be)" column of the needs assessment form (Table 2.8). So needs assessment not only provides the objectives for the methods and means of education, teaching, activities, and learning, it also produces the criteria for evaluation.

In later chapters, methods and techniques for collecting performance data and using them for decision making are provided. Tools and approaches vary from basic and straightforward approaches (such as plotting learner progress in mastery of learning tasks) to complex record keeping on variability of responses and quality for groups of students.

For the near future, when there is a choice, we encourage the simpler methods, for most teachers and administrators do not now have the time and resources to conduct extensive studies on progress and results. With the advent of computer support in the classroom, and our continuing movement toward technological support, the detailed plotting of progress will be easier for educators and students to undertake. Then it will be practical to use many of the important and useful tools available from statistical quality control and quality systems that collect, reduce, analyze, and report information for the continuous improvement of education.

Managing for success: building and using a quality system. Quality management provides the purposes, criteria, and incentives to deliver educational success. With destinations clearly identified, educators and their partners can manage the enterprise: to find what is contributing, what isn't; what to keep, what to change. This success will be continuous, as the school or system consistently improves the quality of its output.

An essential ingredient of QM is a *quality system* that will track performance progress (which is all too often missing from today's educational operations) and provide scientific data to everyone. This is covered extensively in Chapter 5. Based upon valid data, the QM partners can decide what is working and what isn't. Changes can be introduced, continuously, as the organization and everyone in it move toward client satisfaction: ever closer to a successful school, a successful educational system, and an educational enterprise that not only satisfies but also provides a positive return on investment.

The details of creating and using a quality system are provided in Chapters 4 and 5. For now, it is important to realize that the data-based decision-making element of QM relies on collecting and applying valid and useful performance data.

Putting Deming's Principles to Work in Education

A tailoring of Deming's points—with a special emphasis upon results, data-based decision making, payoffs, and contributions—to education includes the following:

1. Create constancy of purpose: The performance and success of learners in and beyond school should be in center focus. Create the vision of what education will deliver, including the measurable specifications for success. Provide a mission objective that will serve as a consistent North Star toward which each person may navigate and contribute. Every person— learners, educators, parents, community members—must work full time to create quality. Half-hearted efforts and one-shot ventures will fail.

2. Adopt a new philosophy: Move from school-centered education to learner-centered success, from teaching subjects to teaching learners, from budget-driven strategies to strategy-driven budgets.

3. Cease dependence on mass inspection to achieve quality: Don't evaluate learners and teachers on the basis of constant grading, testing, and compliance with scheduling. Shift to self-evaluation and self-pacing of learning based upon an overall goal of success in and beyond school. Empower learners to track their own progress and learning means and methods and to change as required. Provide everyone with the

tools to collect and analyze data and convert it to useful information.

4. End the practice of rewarding individual learner classroom performance alone (passing tests, answering oral questions); instead, reward total understanding and overall accomplishments with others.[10] Instead of focusing on course performance, look at holistic accomplishments in and beyond schooling. Deal with educational partners who make the greatest contribution and not with ones who do it most cheaply—put an emphasis on results, not on inputs and processes.

5. Constantly improve the system of teaching, learning, educational support, and service.

6. Institute training on the job. Provide in-service experiences with topics and areas that contribute to competence, empowerment, growth, and self-development. Each person will constantly learn from his or her work, his or her results, and from new research and findings in education and related fields.

7. Institute leadership—substitute it for hierarchical levels of reporting and supervision—by defining and moving constantly toward partnership-derived shared destinations.

8. Drive out fear: Reasonable risks are to be rewarded (with or without success) if they were taken to achieve organizational objectives. Failure is for learning and fixing, not for blaming.

9. Break down barriers between classes, levels, specialties, schools, departments, administration levels.

10. Eliminate slogans, exhortations, and numerical targets.

11. Eliminate work standards (quotas) and management by objective: Mastery and competence are more important than learning (a process), and learning is more important than attendance or compliance. Eliminate rigid, inflexible, and arbitrary curriculum guides, rules, standards, scheduling.

Install and use a system for collecting and using valid performance data.

12. Remove barriers that rob educators, administrators, learners,
and parents of their right to take pride in their accomplishments and contributions to self and others.

13. Institute a vigorous process of results-referenced in-service
education and self-improvement of all staff members. Collect
and use valid data. Use evaluation for improving, not for
blaming.

14. Enroll everyone in the system to work to accomplish the
transformation: Everyone makes their unique contributions
to the shared vision and mission.

So?

We have now set the stage for instituting a QM process and
environment in your school or district. In Chapter 1, we defined the
basic elements of QM and demonstrated that it may be just as
successful in education as it has been in every other area in which it
has been seriously pursued. We also emphasize here two critical
success factors in implementing QM: willingness to move out of your
usual comfort zones and realizing that there are three levels of results
(mega, macro, and micro).

This chapter justified the importance of instituting a QM process
in your school or district. We also provided some of the nuts and bolts
of QM, including a version of Deming's 14 points tailored for education and the steps of setting up a QM activity. Some of the details, not
very flashy but critical, include maintaining an ends focus, writing
objectives in terms of ends and not means, defining needs in terms
of ends—gaps between current ones and desired ones—and not in
terms of missing methods or resources, and needs assessment as the
identification of needs, placing them in priority order, and picking
the most important for action. Also, a description of needs assessment, which identifies possible ways and means (we call them
methods-means) for closing the gaps, was provided. Finally, we
related evaluation to these same basic considerations.

All of this is simply prologue to defining, installing, and using QM in your system. What we deal with next is implementing all of this as part of your "corporate culture"—the way you do education. Ready?

Notes

1. Peter Senge (1990) suggests the term *metanoia* be resurrected as the appropriate label for a shift of mind. This book is about the why's, what's, and how's of such a mind shift in education.

2. Joel Arthur Barker describes this phenomenon clearly and convincingly in his videotape *The Business of Paradigm* in his Discovering the Future Series (ChartHouse Learning Corporation, Burnsville, MN).

3. Rummler and Brache (1990) make a similar point concerning private sector thinking at the macro and micro levels.

4. The issue of taking one's business elsewhere is being seen in the choice/voucher options, which continue to surface at the state as well as the national level. Also, the creation of private schools for delivering a new breed of education is attracting increasing attention. Many nations, including our own, are concerned with the effect of parents sending their children to private schools and what that does to the effectiveness of the system given the ethnic/cultural/values mix of those attending the often beleaguered public institutions.

5. Strong proponents of a results orientation include Mager (1961, 1975), Gilbert (1978), Gilbert and Gilbert (1989), and Kaufman (1972, 1992a, 1992b), to name a few. The earliest clear statement concerning objectives and their results base was Mager's, first as internally published work at Varian Associates and then in influential books published by Fearon.

6. Not who will do the job: That is a means, or process, issue, which has no place in a performance objective.

7. This section builds on earlier work by Kaufman in the area of need, needs assessment, needs analysis, quasi-needs assessment, and system analysis (e.g., Kaufman, 1972, 1988b, 1992a, 1992b; Kaufman & Herman, 1991; Kaufman, Rojas, & Mayer, 1993; Kaufman & Valentine, 1989).

8. There are, curiously, different definitions for *need*. When one uses *need* as a verb ("I 'need' more money." "You 'need' to take a 25%

cut in pay." "I 'need' another triple scotch."), one jumps directly into a means, or solution, without identifying the gaps in results that must be filled. We urge that this gap-in-results definition be used to keep ends and means related. For more on this vital topic, see Kaufman (1992a, 1992b) and Kaufman and Herman (1991).

9. This is termed a *NOM* (needs, opportunities, maintenance) *Assessment* in Kaufman (1992b).

10. As some contemporary researchers point out, we teach and reward individual, private work and accomplishment and ignore the fact that most jobs and social activities require working successfully with others. This cooperative activity is more often punished than facilitated in today's education.

Implementing QM
in Your School or District

Simply wanting quality is not enough. Mobilizing quality teams is not enough. Providing cheerleaders, inspirational statements, posters, and speeches is not enough. Collecting and reporting extensive statistical data are not enough. QM, as much as it is a process, is also a state of mind: an organizational climate and norm.

The environment for thinking, breathing, and delivering quality must be created, nurtured, maintained, and protected. At the same time, everyone in the organization must have the skills and tools to design and deliver continuous improvement of education. The system—your school or district—should provide intrinsic rewards as well as tangible recognition for the contributions to self and others.

What Is Involved?

Change. There, it's been said. Quality management is about change. It is also about energizing, releasing, and encouraging the

54

talents, abilities, and contributions of each and every person in your school or district. It is not blaming, exploiting, or firing.

QM is an ongoing process. It is never complete. It seeks continuous improvement toward perfection.

Here are the general steps involved in setting up a quality environment and instituting QM in your school or district. As we present the steps, recall Deming's 14 points; Joiner's three clusters of "all on one team," "a passion for quality," and "data-based decision making"; as well as Zahn's two additional triangles.

Implementing QM

Change isn't often easy. Armed only with the knowledge that QM is a viable process that has been successful worldwide and your desire to achieve positive change in education, here are the general steps for getting QM started in your school or system. It translates Deming's 14 points into action and results. (There will be more details about these steps as well as useful tools for implementing QM later in the book.) QM participation is only by choice. If people elect not to enroll, then this book and its contents are not for them. We provide specific guidance for defining and achieving QM and continuously improving. There are even some elements that are "musts."

Although changing from old paradigms to new and more useful ones might be, at times, uncomfortable, the wisdom of former Dallas Cowboys coach Tom Landry bears remembering: Coaches get people to do what they don't want to do so that they can achieve what they want to achieve. Continuous improvement is worth the journey for those who understand what's involved in the process and the payoffs. Here are the basic steps for implementing QM:

(1) The decision: Decide to deliver the quality of education that will allow tomorrow's child to be successful and be a good neighbor. This decision should be broad based and involve the opinion leaders in and outside the immediate system. As it becomes possible to do so, include everyone.

The decision to pursue continuous improvement of quality should be driven by intrinsic factors, that is, wanting to do the right thing rather than avoiding punishment or working for any extrinsic reward. After all, we got into education to help learners be successful in school and in life. QM simply provides a rational process for delivering on what we got into the business for in the first place: We got into education to help make *our* world a continuously better place.

QM will only be successful when people at all levels commit to, and participate in, the process. It cannot be delegated by the board or the superintendent. If the bosses (including the school board) don't want it, stop until they join. If they won't be active in it, don't start until they enroll in the quality partnership. QM is motivated action by all involved parties, not talk.

Such blockages in setting up QM, however, should not stop you from applying quality principles everywhere you can—to your work and as you interact with others. Quality can be begun anywhere, but, as you apply it in parts of the organization, work to get everyone on the same quality team. Remember, however, that, as you "breed" quality within your own area and have to interact with others who have not "bought in" to quality, skillful handling will be required; they will probably be using old paradigms and be uncomfortable with what you are doing and why. We will talk more about handling such breakdowns in common purpose in Chapter 6.

Open the QM process to everyone involved in the school or system: teachers, parents, community members, employers, administrators, board members, learners, custodians, support personnel. Prepare a brief statement of the intent of QM and why it will be important for the school, the system, the community, and the learners. Hold an organizational meeting and lay out the details of what QM is, what it isn't, what it will deliver, and what it takes to be successful. Identify the steps and commitments that are required. Be clear, concise, and objective.

Get commitments to participate, and schedule the next steps of the process. Keep all of your promises. Openly address the ones you break and indicate what you have learned from the incidents that will help you to improve in the future.

(2) Commit to quality: Accept the basic principles of QM and commit to put them into practice. Review Deming's 14 points and our educa-

tional version, both in Chapter 2. If the QM team wants to change the educational principles, make certain that they directly relate to Deming's 14 points and that they will deliver learner success in school and in life.

Cluster the resulting QM principles for your school or system into Joiner's clusters (Figure 1.1): all on one team, passion for quality, data-based decision making. Keep these principles in front of your team at all times and apply them constantly.

Pledge to collect and use performance data for continuous improvement. Understand that a quality system must be created and maintained. Acknowledge the existence of evaluation anxiety and address it.

The quality team. Once the commitment has been made to quality, the basic characteristics of quality, and the continuous improvement of education, the partners become the *quality team.* The team enjoys open enrollment. Anyone can join at any time; the more, of course, the better.

After accepting the 14 points (and Joiner's three clusters of "all one team," "scientific approach"—i.e., data-based decision making—and "a passion for quality"), or revising them before accepting them, ask each person on the team to identify:

1. Who are our clients?
2. What would client satisfaction look like, and how would we measure it?
3. What characteristics of the outputs (graduates, completers, and so on) of the educational system would deliver client satisfaction? How would we measure it?
4. What are the building-block results (mastery in courses, abilities, skills, knowledge, and so on) that would deliver what we identified in Steps 3 and 2, above, and how would we measure each?
5. What are the activities (courses, initiatives, activities, and so on) that would deliver the building-block results identified in Step 3, and what are the specifications for each?

6. What resources, including people, facilities, funds, learner entry characteristics, are required to do what was identified in 5 to deliver the results in 4?

7. What must each person do, continuously, to make certain that 6, 5, 4, 3, and 2 happen effectively and efficiently?

8. What data are required for making decisions on how things are progressing, what to keep, what to change, what to stop?

(3) Select the quality level: Select the level at which the QM process will focus: mega, macro, micro. Identify the three possible levels of results (you might use Table 2.3 and Table 2.4) and select the level at which you will focus your QM process. Because QM intends to be client centered, we urge the mega level. (Of course, because choice and willing commitment are crucial, any of the results levels may be selected and the payoffs will be better than if none of the steps in QM was attempted.)

(4) Define the ideal vision: Develop the ideal vision for the QM process and for the school or educational system. The vision for the QM process is targeted on the results level selected. Ask the QM team to develop that vision. Table 3.1 (or a version of it) may be used for obtaining partner vision suggestions.

Summarize vision statements and convert any resources and process statements[1] (e.g., "increasing teacher pay"; "using computers to . . ."; "increase time-on-task") to results statements (e.g., "reduce unwanted teacher turnover to zero"; "teaching techniques used will meet at least 95% of all performance objectives") and add big-picture visions (e.g., "100% of all graduates will get and keep a job in their first or second career choice or be admitted to an accredited college"; "have all learners complete their education within one year of their entering cohorts"). Assure that the vision statements are targeted at the level selected in Step 3 (and revise as required). Again, write ideal visions that include measurable criteria.

The following is an example of *part* of an ideal vision statement:

To achieve total acceptance of the quality of education's graduates and completers; everyone will get and keep a

Table 3.1 A Format for Collecting Visions and Criteria

Ideal Vision/Preferred Future
Describe the world in which you want tomorrow's child to live:

ENDS/Results Criteria
(e.g., 0 use of illicit drugs, no deaths from toxic substances, no species become extinct from human intervention.)

SOURCE: Based on Kaufman (1992b).

job or get accepted into a postsecondary accredited school; there will be no student who fails to graduate or complete a program. Clients' satisfaction will be indicated by surveys showing "good" or better judgments of the district's effectiveness.

(5) Assess needs: Institute the data-based decision-making element by completing a needs assessment. Defining "need" as a gap in results and employing the QM level selected in Step 3, identify gaps between current results and desired ones.

First, identify needs at the level of the ideal vision. Next, identify those for the balance of the QM process (again referring to Figure 1.4). Identify the needs and summarize, using a form similar to that in Table 2.8.

Summarize needs and prioritize them. Get the QM team to select the needs to be addressed and then place them in priority order. Priorities may be set in terms of what it costs to meet the need versus what it will cost to ignore it.

Make certain that the QM partners agree on both the needs and the priorities. If they don't, revise as required. When there is disagreement, additional data collection will usually resolve differences.

(6) Allocate the meeting of the needs: Decide who will be responsible for meeting the selected needs. The QM team may now allocate the needs to be reduced or eliminated (these are now termed *problems*) to team members or groups of team members. Once needs are assigned, it is important that those working on each stay in communication with other team members. Most needs and problems are interlinked, and the relationships among problems and functions can often provide clues for (a) fixing what really is not working well and (b) dealing with underlying causes and not just with surface symptoms. Team members should constantly share their work, findings, and actions.

(7) Identify and select ways to meet needs: Identify possible methods and means (how-to-do-its) and then select the most efficient and effective ones to meet (or reduce) the needs. The quality team members responsible for each need (or cluster of related needs) next identify the possible methods and means that might be available. For each one (or cluster) identified, state the advantages and disadvantages of each.

Table 2.9 provides a possible format for this methods-means analysis. Based on the methods-means analysis, select how each need (or cluster of needs) will be reduced or eliminated. Negotiate with the rest of the system to obtain the methods and means. Because the request for methods and means will be based on gaps in results and on the return on investment for delivering the results, the QM team has a good possibility of successfully negotiating the resources and methods. If management decides not to provide the resources (or come up with a reasonable alternative), they own the responsibility for nonachievement.

(8) Install and institutionalize: Institute continuous improvement in your school or system. Make it a part of everyday life for everyone. QM is not a one-shot affair. It becomes part of the corporate culture and an integral part of everyone's daily activities and work. Here the

passion for quality really comes into central focus (it should always be given your team's constant attention). Everything that is used should improve the quality of what is done and delivered. The insights, experience, and talents of each team member are applied to meeting the needs and moving incessantly toward total quality, toward the ideal vision.

(9) Continuous progress and contribution: Control the QM process and make continuous improvement a part of your culture and environment. Set up a quality system: Collect data, report them to those who require them, and use them to improve. Evaluation—comparing results with intentions—is the constant companion of QM team members. Along the way to client satisfaction, each step compares the results with the intentions. When there is a shortfall, then revisions should be made. Change what should be changed, and continue what's working.

Constantly review your accomplishments with your objectives and renew. Learn from each occurrence. Turn failures into opportunities to learn and make things better. Make QM part of your life.

Now let's look more closely at some of the key elements in installing and institutionalizing QM in your school or system. We will delve a bit more into some additional aspects of the nine QM elements that haven't already had full explanation.

Some Additional Specifics for Installing QM

Steps 1 and 2: The Decision and Commitment to Quality

People make quality a reality. To decide to create quality and make the commitment, the human side of quality should be addressed.

Building the team, building the environment. Nothing is more important to building a team than having common purpose. The vision and mission provide a common North Star toward which to plan, design, develop, deliver, evaluate, and renew.

Identifying and involving the QM partners. The QM partners represent all that has to be used, developed, delivered, and evaluated. They are the team. Quality depends upon their vision, abilities, commitment, and motivation.

QM works best when everyone enrolls in the QM process and purposes, when everyone shares the responsibilities and joys of defining and creating successful contributions. Committing to be part of the QM partnership is not mandatory (Why force someone to do something that they don't want to do?), but the more the better. Provide everyone in your school and system the opportunity to become part of the action. Don't move ahead under these circumstances:

- when executive management (including the board) does not endorse *and* participate
- when significant numbers of potential partners opt not to commit
- when most people are passive about what QM can and will deliver

Creating readiness. Begin to develop empowering relationships within the organization so that people will have partners with whom they would be willing to take the risk of being on a quality improvement team. Begin to demonstrate that accountability is possible within the organization and that it is a positive experience.

Discovering. Have informal teams meet to discover aspects of their work environment that can be improved. Have them talk to their clients to see how well the current system is serving them. Teach the team basic statistical tools and concepts at the point that these tools will help the team to answer questions of interest to them.

Commitments. Just because a person has committed to be a member of the quality team does not mean that he or she will not make any more mistakes. The person may even act in a way that is opposed to quality improvement in the system. The team must develop the ability to inquire about such behavior in a way that does not "make-wrong" the individual involved and in a way that allows this individual to reexamine the choice to be committed to quality improvement in the organization.

Concerns. Everyone on the team will have their own concerns about working on quality improvement. Horror stories from other organizations seeking to do quality improvement, fears of change, grudges, and myriad other concerns will all appear as issues as the group journeys further into quality improvement. Again, the importance of having created empowering relationships within the team is apparent. Each person must feel that the team is a place where all concerns can be voiced honestly without fear of being "made-wrong."

Getting started. First, get commitment through enrolling all the educational partners in defining and building a better future. Start right away to create the quality partnership. Most people will commit when they realize that this is a serious effort—no rubber stamping or doing the same tired things over again under a different label—to which they can contribute. Successful partnerships have the following characteristics:

1. Everyone agrees to work together as they move toward a common destination.
2. Each individual is important and is expected to make a contribution toward the shared effort.
3. Each person provides support and assistance, when asked, to others.
4. Everyone is honest with themselves and each other.
5. Data collection, evaluation, and feedback are used for improving, never for blaming. Everyone learns from mistakes and experience.
6. Objectives are stated clearly, concisely, and without confusion.
7. Means and resources are selected based upon the results to be obtained, not the other way around.

8. There is no limit to what can be accomplished if one doesn't have to own and get credit for his or her ideas.
9. Constant progress and cooperation characterizes everyone's day-to-day efforts and contributions. Everyone looks for opportunities for successful action.

A quality effort builds a partnership with common goals, a cooperative effort, and shared ownership of quality results. Provide each member of the organization with the attributes of a successful partnership and ask if that is the way he or she would like to work. Also share that not everyone will like every decision but all agree that their common destination is worth the required give-and-take.

Schedule a meeting of the partners, and set up the meeting room so that people can interact; a circle or arrangement where people can look directly at each other is the best, but sometimes the group gets too large for that. Let everyone know that this is a meeting of equals and that the choice to participate is optional, not forced. Explain to the educational partners what's involved and what the payoffs will be. This will demonstrate a change in the usual "culture" of planning and doing—from leaders, followers, and hitchhikers to a full partnership among equals.

Depending upon your potential partners, the rationale for wanting to form a QM effort varies. If yours is a school that is already performing well, note that success has been achieved already and that we want to make the school better, day by day. If the organization is in crisis (layoffs, poor test scores, lawsuits, privatization, and so on), then the facts can be laid out—without blame or scapegoating—to let everyone know that they can make the future change from desperation to success.

Let people in your school and/or district know of the potential of forming a quality management team. Discuss what the payoffs will be for them and their educational partners and furnish some radings on the topic.

Why change? Haven't we been through this type of thing before? Change: Even its mention brings distrust. Educators have changed over the years—from one simplistic, one-at-a-time, single quick fix (often mandated) to another or from one superficial idea to another. We mistrust appeals to change because we know that what is offered usually is either counterfeit or cosmetic.

One foundation for foolish changes has been the tenet that educators and parents are ignorant (or lazy) and cannot understand intricate issues and concepts. So, simplistic initiatives are advanced. Another source of irrational change comes from not understanding the size, complexity, and scope of the educational undertaking—we teach subjects and not learners—so that we fragment our responses with a new course here or a slogan there.

Still another source of silly change flows from the failure to link educational resources and processes to in-school and societal clients—results and payoffs that are useful and usable. Not formally linking what we do and deliver to its utility in and for society, we talk about process and hope useful results will follow.

Quality comes about, in part, by everyone being on one team, one team that is headed in the same direction by design rather than by accident. Quality management will take us beyond the past attempts at helping learners help themselves (such as through back-to-basics, local control, competency-based education, computer-assisted instruction, and the like).

When we enroll, with others, in a process of defining and achieving total quality, we will change the way we *think* about education and shift from thinking about efficiency to adding effectiveness and usefulness of results and contributions to the education soup as well. Rhetoric in education has too long hinted at results, while the actual practice has often regressed into just putting new labels on process- and resources-related activities. Useful performance has to take center stage. Quality management depends upon data-based decision making, and the data must be relate to ends, results, consequences, and payoffs.

Schools are not factories stamping out identical devices from standardized raw materials. The most difficult difference between education and factories is that schools must take all who come to them while factories may generally select their raw materials. In this regard, education is more like the private sector service arena: a dry cleaner or a physician cannot choose who walks in the doors.

But the fact remains: We promise to deliver useful outputs, that is, useful to both our learners and to the society that pays for the graduates. Education performs a vital and constantly modifying function in a changing world. Quality management and continuous improvement are important endeavors for education and educators if we are to be responsive and responsible.

QM and survival of educational organizations. How can any organization fail to realize that external clients must be satisfied and that satisfaction comes from delivering a quality output time after time after time? Will a computer software company survive if its programs are in error 35% of the time? What about a commuter railroad that failed to arrive at its destinations in one third of all departures?

What are the survival chances of an organization that provides services—such as education—at its convenience, only affords choices of products that it wants to make available without consulting the clients concerning their requirements, and charges whether or not the client wanted or benefited from the services? Are increasingly strident calls for educational reform, restructuring, and "choice" based upon citizens and politicians being ready to give up on education as we now know it? Quality management, sensibly and sensitively conceived and implemented, can assure an educational system that is responsive and responsible, one that is more likely to survive as it continuously improves.

There are at least two good reasons to apply quality management. First, it is the right thing to do. If you don't intend to serve the client well, what do you have in mind? Second, you and your organization aren't likely to survive if you don't. Organizational change expert Daryl Conner (in press) notes that organizations, as well as their QM efforts, usually fail because they don't have the base drive for survival: They don't see themselves as standing on a burning oil-drilling platform, or they believe they are wearing an asbestos suit. He notes that change must be beyond just the comfortable. Major change must be driven by an ability to move beyond one's desire not to have one's expectations and life disrupted.

There are some reasons not to implement quality management:

Don't do it if it is just a fad or because others are doing it.

Don't do it if you are not going to model it and sponsor it through the tough times as well as the joyful ones.

Don't do it if it is going to be delegated to others to get done.

Don't do it if you think it's a program rather than a transformation of how you do business.

Don't do it if you expect quick results.

QM must be a way of organizational life. Everyone should want to do it for the simple purposes of surviving and contributing. There are no shortcuts to quality; there are no quick fixes. Quality processes should be initiated because they are vital to organizational survival and contribution, because there are no other rational choices.

Getting QM accepted. We have to change and improve, and we must get our partners to agree both on the demand for change (and improvement) as well as on becoming partners in the process.

Choosing to be successful, not just comfortable. We have choice in how we view our educational world. Is it one where simply working harder will get us demanded results, or is it one where we must work smarter? It is our choice to open ourselves to responsible and responsive change, in spite of the way that we always have done things, to move out of our comfort zones when reality rears its head. And one of the first things to jostle our comfort zones is direction setting: Where are we now headed in education, where should we be going, and who is the client of education?

We have good reason to change: Making the case for those who do not yet agree.[2] Education is under attack. Either our partners realize it or someone can help them accept reality. As we noted in Chapter 1, the demand for change is coming at us even from our friends. Business as usual will not suffice.

Our troubles don't always come from bad or deceitful people, selfish unions, uncaring teachers, stupid administrators, quick-fix boards of education, unfeeling legislators, political revolutionaries. The troubles are more than intolerable racism, sexism, or exploitation, although these elements can cause situations to deteriorate even more.

Legislated and conventional approaches to "fixing" education seem to ebb and flow like the tides, rushing in only to recede and be replaced by another wave. They surge from teacher-centered to learner-centered instruction; curriculum reforms move from student-responsive to a common core (and back again) and from centralized administration to local control (Cuban, 1990).[3]

We have been tinkering with education and nibbling around the edges of true change. We suspect appeals for so-called change because the change is often either counterfeit or superficial. Suggestions for "true reform" vary from tinkering with the hours of school and teacher's pay to changing our form of government! Transformational change, and quality, will come from the people involved, not from what is imposed from the outside.

Deming and his students agree that most workers are doing their best; blaming or exhorting them will yield little. So, simplistic answers and methods—quick fixes—will yield little. As we noted earlier, working harder won't make us more successful; we are already doing as good a job of conventional education as can be done if we don't challenge our basic assumptions about schools, schooling, and how we create education.

Spending more money on more teachers, more teacher aides, and more administrators will not be either successful or salable. We have to involve our human resources in building—together—a team to deliver quality, which will delight the clients as well as make a positive contribution to our shared world. People are key, and their commitment to continuous improvement is essential.

Making useful results happen. Caring alone is not enough. We must shift our preoccupation with resources and processes that often fail us (Kirst & Meister, 1985; Osborne & Gaebler, 1992) to a primary focus on results, payoffs, and positive consequences. We must stop dealing with single-variable/single-issue responses to our caring about students and their future. We must change: revitalize our schools, rethink our goals and purposes, and restructure our educational system so that it works smarter—effectively and efficiently. We must shift from a preoccupation with resources and methods to a concern for quality. We have to be accountable for quality: the first time, every time, with no rejects.

Step 3: Select the Quality Level

Quality may be improved at any organizational level: mega, macro, or micro. The selection and commitment must be formal. Sooner or later, the mega level must be included—Critical Success Factor 2—but start where you can.

Asking and committing to answer the educational questions for QM. Earlier, in Table 2.3, we provided the basic menu of questions a QM team could ask and answer. Review these with the QM team and decide on the following:

1. Which of the questions can we afford to ignore or assume the answer?
2. Which of the questions do we now *not* formally attend to?
3. Which of the questions do we commit to answer and deliver on?

The questions, when considering commitment, may be framed as shown in Figure 3.1.

Usually, most QM partnerships attend to Questions 2-7 (more on dealing with Question 1 in Chapter 4). Remember that the choice is to be made strictly by the partners. Given the full menu, the choice becomes the option of the team, along with the responsibility for what they choose not to accomplish.

Counseling, coaching, and consulting as an integral part of QM. People helping people: Total quality management gets many people outside of their comfort zones, and they can help each other by counseling, coaching, and consulting. Help comes in different ways for different people. We have found all three of these activities to be valuable and urge you to make use of them.

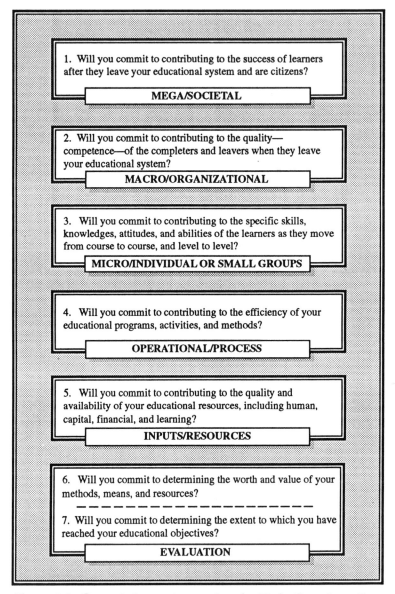

Figure 3.1. Committing to Answering the Right Questions: Seven Basic Questions All Educators Should Ask (and Answer)
SOURCE: Kaufman (1992b).

Helping yourself and helping others. We are in education together, and QM is a vehicle for helping ourselves and others at the same time. It can be applied to any process in one's personal or professional life.

The importance of a common destination. One cohesive force in team effort, management, and contribution is having a shared vision and destination—Step 4. At the core of QM is this shared destination and a shared way of getting quality: all on one team, a passion for quality, and data-based decision making.

Eliminating blame. Results should be compared with objectives and the discrepancies identified. The results of evaluation should be used only for fixing and never for blaming. An essential element of QM is to drive out fear, eliminate blaming, eliminate make-wrongs within the team when discussing results. Continuous improvement depends upon fixing the system rather than blaming the people.

When change gets uncomfortable. Listen to others; don't just wait to talk. What do their comments tell you about their commitments and concerns? QM environment and process depend upon everyone buying in to the purposes and procedures, so it is worth the time to have a dialogue about what QM is, what it can and should deliver, and how it is good for everyone. Not everyone else's concerns are wrong or ill-founded, so concerns are worth listening to and dealing with. Sometimes you can reason with the objectors; sometimes they will provide some insights you have missed.

Change, any change, is often seen as an implied criticism of the status quo and the people who are part of the system. After all, if they were doing things right, why would you want to initiate a QM process? Be aware of this possibility and bring it up very early in the QM process initiation. Be clear that QM is intended to make a good thing better and to make certain we all—together—survive and contribute. You might want to share with the QM partners some of the educational change research and history covered in Chapter 1.

Some people will be direct about their concerns, and this should both be encouraged and provide the opportunity to reason together. One way to negotiate is to write the concerns down and note whether they deal with ends or means. If they are focused on means, simply (and without being sardonic) ask: "If you did (or got) this, what result would we want?" Asked a few times (as required), especially when the objections and responses are written down, can bring about the shifts.

Sometimes the objections are passive. These are often seen as snide comments (often whispered to a neighbor) or statements such as "you just don't know how the real world works." Don't get angry, and certainly don't get into a power game. Be calm and clear. Listen and invite people to list both their concerns and how they would overcome them. When they (and people almost always do) propose a means (more money, more teachers, more aides, less playground duty) ask: "If you did (or got) this, what result would we want?" Let them know that an important part of the QM process is "data-based decisioning" and that the needs assessment will provide that important data. Patience pays off.

Choice. Remember, at all times, that you and all of the QM partners have choice. All can become or can continue to be active participants in defining and delivering quality, or some might opt to "go along, but unconvinced" or even decide not to take part.

Nonparticipation is unfortunate, but it is better to have that declared and in the open; then you can work to demonstrate to nonparticipants that what the others are doing and accomplishing is worth their attention and commitment.

Step 4: Define the Ideal

Preparing the school vision: What kind of organization do you wish to work with and help create? If successful schools are to be fashioned, the QM team will have to do it. A major element in QM is defining the vision.

Identifying a vision: What would we like to deliver? And to whom? A vision, for QM activity, identifies who is to be the primary client and beneficiary of what we do and deliver, and exactly what we should deliver. A vision provides our destination—a common purpose toward which everyone in the organization can steer. It is an "ideal objective." Thus a vision is like any other objective; it precisely states where we want to go and how to tell when we've arrived.

A hallmark of QM is that the client should be satisfied, delighted, with what is delivered to her. Our educational system (or our school) should intend to deliver quality and thus must define what that quality is. A vision for a QM[4] effort in education might be as follows:

> To achieve total acceptance of the quality of education's graduates and completers; everyone will get and keep a job and/or get accepted into a postsecondary accredited school; there will be no student who fails to graduate or complete a program. Clients' satisfaction will be indicated by continuing financial support at the same level or increased levels.

Notice that this vision statement speaks to ends and does not include any means or how-to-do-its. It forms the basis of a statement that precisely identifies what results the school or system will deliver: the mission objective.

Writing the mission objective: Where you are headed and how you will know when you have arrived. A mission objective sets the direction for everything that follows. It is more than an intent ("improve the quality of education") or an inspirational statement ("total quality for everyone by the end of the decade"). It is a clear and unmistakable declaration of where we are going and how we can tell when we've arrived.

A *mission statement* provides a simple direction without specific criteria for measuring our success ("improve education," "quality learning for all"). A mission statement is an intent that is measurable on a nominal or ordinal scale.

A *mission objective* adds very precise criteria to a mission statement that are measurable on an interval or ratio scale, such as "there will be no learners who graduate from Janice High School who do not get and keep a job for at least 6 months." A mission objective is a mission statement plus precise and exact standards by which to determine success:

Mission Statement + Precise Criteria = Mission Objective

All objectives should have clear, unmistakable, and precise criteria for both guiding us to get to that destination as well as providing criteria for an evaluation level of accomplishment. The ABCD criteria and format provided in Tables 2.6 and 2.7 are useful for developing any objective, including a mission objective.

In their most powerful use, mission objectives derive from the ideal vision:

Ideal Vision → Educational Mission Objective

A Motorola executive, commenting on how critical the choice of mission objectives is, noted that the performance measures chosen will channel the organization toward its future. As always, "What gets assessed, gets stressed."[5]

Step 5: Assess Needs

Doing a needs assessment for QM. As we noted in Chapter 2 and earlier in this chapter, a *need* is a gap in results, a discrepancy between current results and desired ones. Further, we defined a *needs assessment* as the process of identifying needs, placing them in priority order, and selecting the most important for reduction or elimination.

The same needs assessment processes we described in Chapter 2 are appropriate for QM. Needs should be identified at each of the levels of results. A more complete format is provided in Table 2.8. Table 3.2 provides a basic format for doing a QM needs assessment.

It provides a basic summary form that summarizes needs data—current results and desired results—and identifies *possible* methods and means (which often are confused with needs). Gaps in results, needs, are listed. Until a need is related to a means, the item remains in the "possible" means column. This format helps to keep needs and solutions separate but related.

Note that the gaps in results may be seen in terms of the linked elements shown in Figure 1.3. Another way to visualize QM needs assessment is in terms of the basic components shown in Figure 3.2.

Table 3.2 A Basic Needs Assessment Summary Format for an Educational QM Activity

Current Results	Possible Means	Desired Results

It is important to identify gaps in results, not discrepancies in methods or resources (called "quasi needs").

Gaps in results—needs—may be identified at each results level of the QM process. Figure 3.2 shows the results parts of a QM needs assessment. Needs at the *outcomes, outputs,* and *products* levels may be identified.

Two varieties of needs data. Two types of needs data should be included. One type is called "hard" data, which are results that can be independently verified. The other is personal, nonindependently verifiable perceptions, which we term *soft* data.

Although it is tempting to collect only opinion data (ask people what their needs are) or to harvest only performance-based data, both are required. People's perceptions are their reality. If they do not state their beliefs and values, and open themselves to change, then we are doomed to forever deal with conflicts in means (solutions and how-to-do-its).

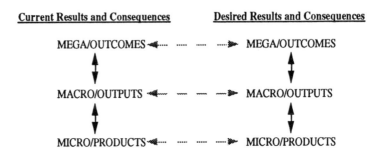

Figure 3.2. A Needs Assessment May Be Done at Each Results Level of the QM Process: Mega/Outcomes, Macro/Outputs, Micro/Products

However, if we often only collect convenient "hard" data, we might miss important blank spaces (see Figure 2.1) in our educational system, which are not part of the data system. Thus both varieties of data are important, should be collected and used, and should agree before one goes ahead with any changes.

A review of the eight steps of a QM-related needs assessment.[6] Some educational agencies have already embarked on a process they call needs assessment. In many cases, if they have collected results-referenced data, what is available can be useful in the QM process. Most available needs assessment data are not related to ends, however, but to means. Here are the basic steps of doing a needs assessment so that you (a) could suggest these to your existing needs assessors and/or (b) follow them as you do a QM needs assessment:

(1) Decide to implement data-based decision making based on the results of a needs assessment. The information from a well-conceived needs assessment allows you to justify your destination. Needs assessment information will allow the QM team to develop a plan—an action blueprint.

(2) Select the needs assessment and planning level: micro, macro, or mega. Needs may be assessed at any of these three levels. Choosing

the micro or macro level assumes that the contributions of those results will be responsive to the mega level: client and societal requirements.

(3) Identify the needs assessment associates from among the total QM partnership. A needs assessment's usefulness depends on choosing the correct partners to guide the process and to "own" it when it is completed. A QM initiative could fail because alienated or unrepresented/underrepresented people may not believe that an imposed change as part of QM, no matter how rational, might benefit them.

Select planning partners who are representative of their constituencies. A stratified random sample of each partner group will provide appropriate representation.

Need has several conventional meanings. Make sure that all the partner groups are working with the same gaps-in-results definition. Use both "hard" and "soft" data to assure an accurate identification of needs.

People will supply judgments concerning perceived needs; these "sensed needs," or feelings, are termed *soft* data. Sensed needs often provide perceived reality and sensitivity to issues of values and preferences about current problems and consequences.

The QM process also requires data concerning gaps in performance: hard data concerning both human and organizational performance. Hard data might include external results (outcomes) such as continued funding, school system image, graduation and/or job placement rates, numbers of completers and leavers with positive credit ratings, quality of community life, and the like. Hard data also might include internal system performance indicators (outputs and products) such as graduation, licensures, dropouts, class standings, absenteeism, morale, organizational climate, delivered services, successful lawsuits, and complaints.

Together, the sensed needs from the implementers, recipients, and external society/clients plus the performance-based data provide the needs assessment data.

(4) Assure the QM/needs assessment partners' participation. Partners must be active contributors. Reveal to each the expectations, required time commitments, required products, and level of contributions.

State how much you will support them—with funds, travel, data, materials, support services, and the like. Be clear concerning how their inputs will be used.

After getting commitments from the partners, design and schedule the first meeting. Alternative methods include face-to-face activities or could use written surveys, delphi techniques, teleconferencing, or computer interfaces. If someone is not participating, replace him or her.

(5) Obtain acceptance of the QM needs assessment level. Share with the partners the three QM levels: mega, macro, and micro (see Step 2). Get them to commit to a level. It is important that all partners know the scope of the needs assessment and have a common set of understandings and expectations.

Inform them they will have to decide which gaps to close first. Recall that there may be three kinds of needs assessments—one relating to each of the three types of results.

Needs analysis consists of determining the reasons for the gaps in results and finding the causes of the inability for one level (e.g., products), when aggregated, to deliver required outputs. Needs analysis rationally proceeds from an assessment of needs: How does one analyze something if it has not been first identified and selected?

(6) Collect both internal and external needs data. Scanning for useful data is accomplished both outside of the educational agency (What happens to learners after they graduate? Drop out? Get further education? Are they working and earning their own way?) and within it (How are grades? Test results? Truancy? Graffiti?). Internal needs data concern performance discrepancies within an organization, and external needs data concern performance discrepancies of your clients and their world.

When collecting data on internal performance, examine two information sources: the perceptions of the planning partners and the actual performance discrepancies collected from objective observations.

Collect partners' perceptions concerning performance discrepancies by using a variety of tools and methods ranging from face-to-face meetings to remote data collection methods such as rating scales, questionnaires, delphi technique, nominal group technique, structured interviews, or some paper-and-pencil assessments.[7] The sensed needs—soft data—of the partners will supply data concerning performance discrepancies they feel are important.

Table 3.3 provides a sample format for collecting "what is" and "what should be" data. Table 3.4 provides a checklist for considerations when developing a needs assessment questionnaire.

In designing or selecting needs-sensing data collection instruments, assure that they pose the correct questions without bias; don't frame questions to get desired responses. Items should be keyed to possible need areas. Make certain the instrument and its questions focus responses on results, not on resources (inputs) or methods and techniques (processes). Also be sure the questions cover the array of needs without imposing on the respondents long and complex questionnaires. The data collection instruments must be valid (measuring that which they are really intended to measure), reliable (measuring the same thing consistently), and unbiased (not measuring consistently too high or too low).

Collecting internal performance data is usually straightforward. Most educational organizations have a lot of hard data; you only have to identify what you want and then locate it. Useful data areas might include absenteeism, course completions/failures/repeats, grades, test scores, truancy, dropouts, graduation rates, vocational occupational specialty certifications, criterion-referenced test results, standardized test results, job placements, counseling cases closed, audit exceptions, ethics violations, accidents, on-site fatalities, grievances, in-service training courses completed, certified competencies, sick leave, work samples.

If the planning partners have chosen the mega assessment level, you will have to collect external performance data. When doing so, you frequently will find useful information available both within and external to the organization. Some examples are data concerning parent and citizen perceptions and satisfaction, on-the-job evaluations, complaints, state and national awards, student arrests and convictions, successful lawsuits, and levels of funding over time.

(7) Resolve differences among the QM partners. It is important to have solid agreement between sources of data. Otherwise, the part-

Table 3.3 A Format for Collecting "Soft" Data: Perceptions of
Needs by Comparing "What Is" and "What Should Be"

For each item, please check the category which you think best represents education in our
school/district. Please make a check for each of two dimensions: WHAT IS (our current performance)
and WHAT SHOULD BE (our desired performance). To help you in making your choice, you might
think of an incident which you have personally observed or experienced.

WHAT IS						WHAT SHOULD BE				
SA	A	N	DA	SDA		SA	A	N	DA	SDA
					Our students are good citizens (no crime, bullying, illegal drug use, etc.)					
					Every learner graduates or gets a vocational certificate					
					Students enter at all levels ready to learn					
					Our former students are good citizens (no crime, bullying, illegal drug use, etc.)					
					Our students get jobs					
					Our students get jobs they want					
					Our learners not only get jobs, they perform well and keep employed					
					Our learners, when they desire, go on to further education					
					Our learners who go on to further education complete programs or degrees					
					Parents are satisfied with the results of education delivered here					
					Community members are satisfied with the results of education delivered here					
					Learners are satisfied with the results of education delivered here					
					Quality--concern for learner success and colleague cooperation--is part of the way we do things around here					
					Parents are part of the educational system and are active participants in their children's success					
					Learners' performance on tests and other assessments is acceptable					
					Teachers and professional staff go out of their way to help all learners					
					Our graduates and completers are self-sufficient					
					Our graduates and completers are good neighbors					
					Etc.					

NOTE: There are both ends-related items and means-related ones. The
means-related data, dealing with quasi needs, will be useful when doing a
needs analysis. *Key:* SA = strongly agree, A = agree, N = neutral, DA = disagree, and SDA = strongly disagree.

Table 3.4 Considerations for Developing a Needs Assessment Questionnaire

_____	1. Make certain that the questions are about results, not about processes or inputs.
_____	2. Ask about perceptions of gaps in results for both dimensions— what is and what should be.
_____	3. Ask about the three levels of needs:

  • External (Mega)
  • Organizational contributions (Macro)
  • Building-block results (Micro)

_____	4. Assure validity and reliability.
_____	5. Make the questionnaire long enough to get reliable responses, but short enough that people will actually respond.
_____	6. Use an approach that makes it clear to respondents exactly what is wanted. People usually don't want to write long answers, so a checklist will reduce their burden while making the questionnaire easier to score.
_____	7. Don't ask questions that reveal, directly or indirectly, a bias. Don't use the data collection vehicle to set up the responses you really want.
_____	8. Ask several questions about each concern in different ways, to assure reliability in the responses. Basing any decision on answers to one question is risky.
_____	9. Try out the data-collection instrument on a sample group to identify problems in meaning, coverage, and scorability. Revise it as required.

When collecting performance (or "hard") data:

_____	10. Make certain the data collected relate to important issues for which you want answers.
_____	11. Assure yourself that the data you use are collected correctly and that the methods used for gathering them and reporting are free of bias.
_____	12. Assure yourself that the data are based upon enough observations to make them reliable, not a one-shot happening.
_____	13. Make certain that the data can be independently verified and cross-checked.

ners, and the interests they represent, won't perceive the needs assessment data as useful and they won't accept the results. Where there isn't accord, initiate further fact-finding and/or reeducate the needs assessment partners so they can agree.

Figure 3.3 shows a process for merging the two types of data and deciding on the areas for collection of additional information. When disagreement lingers, consider revisiting the historical context and the futures data to provide a frame of reference concerning "what was," "what is," "what will be," and "what could be" before finally selecting "what should be."

Again, most disagreements stem from (a) confusing ends and means, (b) insisting on a favored means and not first defining gaps in results (needs) before finding an appropriate means, and/or (c) power games. Bring these possibilities up with the planning partners and list the existing "needs." Make up a simple chart with the "needs" in a first column and then two other columns marked "ends" and "means." Have the group fill out the chart; they will usually notice that some premature "means" have slipped in. List the needs to be prioritized and addressed. Table 3.5 provides still another possible *macro-level* format for needs assessment.

(8) List agreed-upon needs and their priorities. Placing the agreed-upon needs in priority order involves asking and answering:

"What does it cost to meet the need?" and
"What does it cost to ignore the need?"

Each of the QM partners should participate in the prioritizing and agree with the final list.

Steps 6 and 7: Allocate the Meeting of Needs and Identify and Select Ways of Meeting Needs

Allocating assignment of meeting needs among the partners. Partners work together toward a shared vision and mission. Each person in a school or district brings unique skills, knowledge, and abilities. Each person can and should make a unique contribution to the quality effort.

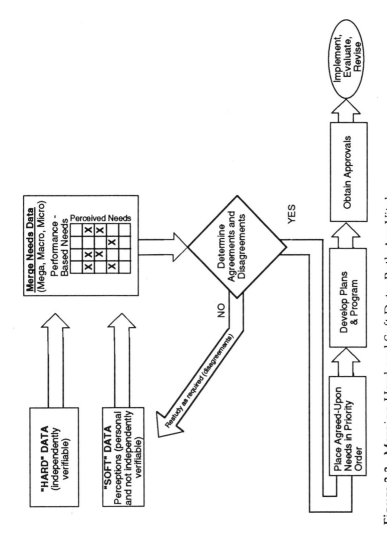

Figure 3.3. Merging Hard and Soft Data: Both Are Vital
SOURCE: Based on Kaufman (1988a).

83

Table 3.5 A Needs Assessment Summary Format for Conventional—Macro-Level—Quality Management

Current Results	Possible Means	Required Results	Ideal Vision Element	NEED LEVEL	
				Macro	Micro

NOTE: A means should remain in the second column until it is selected to meet one or more needs.

84

Based upon who is best qualified to meet an identified need (and related problem), the quality team should agree on who is to do what and when. It is important that the team knows and agrees with the assignments to (a) be clear about what each person is attending to and (b) understand possible interrelationships between their role and responsibility (e.g., communication skills, social skills) and others' roles and responsibilities (e.g., social studies, automotive repair). Instead of continuing to teach subjects and not learners, a quality team may develop synergies among activities (e.g., automobile mechanics must be able to clearly communicate problems and situations to customers and fellow workers; they must also be able to get along with colleagues and families).

Each person can make a contribution. And each person's contributions must integrate with those of others to assure that what we develop and deliver in education will be useful to both the individual learners and the society for which they are being prepared.

Identifying and selecting the best tools and techniques to achieve quality. Tools and techniques are the how-to-do-its and resources that may be used to get results. They may be sensibly selected after we know (a) the needs to be reduced or eliminated and (b) the objectives for what has to be delivered in the system.

This is the part of the QM process most people feel comfortable with—doing. Because of the comfort associated with "doing" methods and means and the discomfort associated with a needs assessment, partners must be vigilant that the team does not move prematurely from needs assessment to *selecting* methods and means. Table 2.9 provides a methods-means analysis format. Fill it out with your QM partners.

After identifying the possible methods and means to reduce or eliminate needs, then you are ready to select your methods. Basically, one selects a method or a means by finding the most effective and efficient alternative. There are a number of tools and techniques for selection, including the following:

- systems analysis
- operations research
- planning, programming, budgeting system (PPBS)

- simulation, gaming, queuing
- relevance trees
- delphi technique
- nominal group technique
- polling
- cross-impact analysis
- cycle analysis

We don't go into these techniques here. We suggest you review Chapter 7 of *Planning Educational Systems* (Kaufman, 1988a) and use the references there.

Step 8: Install and institutionalize

We cannot overemphasize the importance of making quality a part of the corporate culture. Everyone must "live" quality and be all on one quality team (to achieve the ideal vision), have a passion for quality (again, getting continuously closer to the ideal vision), and make data-based decisions. Quality has to be seen and acted upon as "the way we do education around here."

Installing and institutionalizing require patience. Because this is a process, however, the tools of QM can be applied to it. This application will identify parts of the organization in which installation is proceeding smoothly and parts where additional attention is required.

Step 9: Continuous Progress and Contribution

An essential aspect of making the continuous improvement process truly continuous is to remain consistent in basing decisions on data. The data must always be used for improving the processes, for identifying opportunities for actions that will improve the processes. Never use it for blaming.

Several factors contribute to keeping the quality team together and keeping things moving. When data are gathered, it is important that they be analyzed at once and that actions be proposed on the basis of this analysis. Not doing this will discourage the team and make it reluctant to take the risk of gathering data in the future.

Another factor that will contribute to continuous progress is making sure that all individuals involved see breakdowns as possibilities in disguise rather than events to be covered up or blamed on other parties. Our society's conventional, knee-jerk reaction to breakdown is most detrimental to the continuous improvement of quality. Breakdowns are seen as events to be avoided. In the quest for quality improvement, exactly the opposite attitude is essential. If we are seeking to improve a system, it is a certainty that a breakdown of some magnitude will eventually occur. A thorough analysis of this breakdown from the perspective of what can be learned from it will help us to improve the system.

Teams must learn to avoid responding to breakdowns by engaging in conversations about who is at fault or to blame. These conversations about fault and blame only serve to elicit higher levels of defensiveness and do not serve to identify what can be learned from the breakdown. Dealing with breakdowns is discussed more extensively in Chapter 6.

The nine elements suggested here (or you may well develop your own set) will deliver total quality and continuous improvement:

1. Make the decision.
2. Commit to quality.
3. Select the quality level.
4. Define the ideal.
5. Assess needs.
6. Allocate the meeting of needs.
7. Identify and select ways of meeting needs.
8. Install and institutionalize the process.
9. Continue progress and contribution.

The methods and means for assuring total quality and continuous improvement are found through the commitment, talent, and relentless contribution of a quality team working together to define and deliver total quality. It is practical, possible, and rewarding.

Awards—Recognizing Quality—
and Beyond Awards

Organizations are increasingly anxious to show themselves and their clients that they are "quality-oriented" operations. Several awards and types of recognition have become available. Applying for an award allows people to get serious about what it takes to think and deliver quality. Winning an award is cause for celebration, for it gives notice that quality is "done here."

Winning a quality award is not always the same as delivering consistent quality. The pursuit of quality requires perseverance and quality doesn't survive without constant development and delivery. Educational agencies can be expected to seek quality certification in coming years, and they should realize that quality is more than getting "tickets punched" or winning a one-time certificate.

In fact, it is critical that the desire for an award not be the driving force behind a quality improvement initiative. If desire for the award is the driving force, then winning the award becomes more important than serving customers, and, if the award is won, the organization is hard pressed to keep the quality improvement systems in place after the goal has been achieved.

Usually only granted in Japan, the Deming Award is being sought by many organizations. Its criteria are relatively general as compared with those of other certification procedures. More popular and recognized in the United States is the Baldrige Award.

The Malcolm Baldrige Award. QM works everywhere it is genuinely used in business and industry. The U.S. Commerce Department's Malcolm Baldrige Award is coveted. By winning it, each employee and manager, each secretary and vice president, can take pride in being distinguished as delivering total quality—for achieving client satisfaction. The distinction can be financially rewarding as well as a source of deep pride.

The weighted criteria for the 1992 Baldrige Award, based on a total of 1,000 points, are leadership (90 points), information and analysis (80), strategic quality planning (60), human resource development and management (150), management of process quality (140), quality and operational results (180), and customer focus and satisfaction (300). While these criteria may not all be clearly results referenced, the intentions are clear: client satisfaction through high quality outputs.

The ISO (International Standards Organization) 9000 Series.[8] These standards are growing in influence in both industry and education. Designed to be an "effective building block for achieving TQM" (Det norske Veritas Industry, n.d.-a), this series includes the elements of ISO 9000 (quality management and quality assurance standards), ISO 9001 (quality systems: model for quality assurance in design/ development, production, installation, and servicing), ISO 9002 (quality systems: model for quality assurance in production and installation), ISO 9003 (quality systems: model for quality assurance in final inspection and testing), and ISO 9004 (quality management and quality system elements).

True to its billing, the ISO 9000 series attends to certification of compliance with published standards and manuals and with providing evidence, which can be independently audited, of following published guidelines and demonstrating required quality standards. While, in the main, ISO 9000 attends to procedures and compliance, there are some inferential links possible to micro-, macro-, and even a few mega-level results and consequences (H. Mayer, personal communication, August 1992). The ISO 9000 series can provide guidance on stating, documenting, and tracking the required processes to achieve quality in education.

Beyond winning awards. More and more organizations are striving to win an envied Malcolm Baldrige or a Deming Award (see DeYoung, 1990; Galagan, 1991; Imai, 1986) and/or receiving accredition for compliance with ISO 9000 (Det norske Veritas Industry, n.d.-b). Even more important than winning an award (or winning the approval of others for our efforts), we should be pursuing quality simply because the results and payoffs will be worthwhile for their own sake; we don't have to chase someone else to accomplish what is correct and useful. We had better convert from extrinsic to intrinsic motivation (Senge, 1990).

Our domestic survival and quality of life seem to hinge on making quality our primary focus and first accomplishment. U.S.

companies are finding that, to do business in European markets, they will have to demonstrate how they meet the 20 criteria for quality specified by the ISO 9000 series of standards (Marquardt et al., 1991).

Sometimes Quality Initiatives
Get Things Out of Balance:
How to Keep QM From Failing

Not all quality efforts are successful. Even organizations that have won the coveted Baldrige, meet the criteria for ISO 9000 standards, or bagged the Deming Award find themselves shifting their quality gears or just burning out. This doesn't have to happen.

There are several ways for a QM process to fail. One is to expend all efforts on winning an award, getting "your tickets punched" instead of doing the right thing—supplying added value for your clients. If you spend your time and efforts on jumping hurdles to get certified, you might (a) get locked into delivering things that meet certification criteria and not continuously improving or (b) forget the overall purpose for quality management and continuous improvement. Another way to fail is to spend your time collecting performance data and not achieve the QM balance among all on one team, a passion for quality, and data-based decision making. Continuous improvement is a moment-by-moment, day-by-day activity that requires balance.

An Ernst and Young study of quality management initiatives, *Best Practices Report,* indicated that many appear to be floundering from a lack of focus. Some companies institute broad training programs followed by attempts to implement vast numbers of new procedures immediately. These companies tend to get stalled before the investment has shown any return. They appear to regard QM as a program to adopt rather than as a transformational shift in the organization's philosophy.[9]

QM is a means to an end. The end has to be the success and survival of our clients, ourselves, and our world. If you forget that, QM will fall short of its full promise.

Some quality-minded companies reflect an awareness of this. For example, the Quality Policy of Milliken & Company, winner of the Baldrige Award in 1989, includes the statement:

> We will continually strive to provide innovative, better and better quality products and services to enhance our customers' continued long-term profitable growth by understanding and exceeding their requirements and anticipating their future expectations. (Milliken & Company, 1990)[10]

Notes

1. Consider retaining resource and process statements and holding them for later when possible methods and means to achieve desired results will be considered.

2. Based, in part, on Kaufman (1992b).

3. Regardless of the explanations offered in the literature for successions of these cyclical changes, they all seem to overlook a common element: agreement among the educational partners on what education should deliver. If education "is the solution," what's the problem? We believe that one of the basic difficulties with defining and delivering educational success is not in the dedication of teachers or parents but in the basic lack of agreement on what the objectives of education are—what education should deliver. Several books, including Kaufman (1992a, 1992b) and Kaufman and Herman (1991), deal with how to "fix" this.

4. In the next chapter, we will suggest some additional considerations to add to QM to make it even more powerful.

5. These comments were made by Bill Smith in his presentation on Motorola's prize-winning quality improvement program at the University of Wisconsin—Madison symposium, "Problem-Driven Case Studies in Quality Improvement," in November 1991.

6. These are summarized, with permission, from the following books: R. Kaufman (1988a), *Planning Educational Systems: A Results-Based Approach* (Lancaster, PA: Technomic); R. Kaufman and J. Herman (1991), *Strategic Planning in Education: Rethinking, Restructuring, Revitalizing* (Lancaster, PA: Technomic); R. Kaufman (1992a),

Strategic Planning Plus: An Organizational Guide (Newbury Park, CA: Sage).

    7. We will not go into the how-to-do-its of these techniques. Basic textbooks on the topic are readily available.

    8. The U.S. equivalent to the ISO 9000 series is ANSI/ASQC Q90-Q94.

    9. *The Wall Street Journal* (May 13, 1992, p. B1).

    10. We will address the shortcomings of quality policies such as this one in Chapter 4.

Quality Management Plus

QM+ Delivers More

Do Most Quality Programs
Go Far Enough?

When client satisfaction is good but not good enough. All organizations are means to societal ends, and they all have external clients. Education's client list is long. It includes just about everyone in our society: learners, parents, teachers, administrators, board members, governments, businesses, media, taxpayers, neighbors.

Some of these are internal clients, those who work and operate within the educational system. Other educational clients are external to the system. They are the ones who pay for education and become the employers and neighbors of our educational outputs.

All clients are important; all are stakeholders; and all must be satisfied with what we use, do, and deliver. Meeting educational clients' requirements is a tall order!

Usually, the most vocal clients, and those with the most political clout, are the external ones: board members, governments, businesses, media, taxpayers, neighbors. To keep those external clients satisfied, our schools and systems have to provide added value: a continuous positive return on investment. External clients have to know that they are getting what they pay for and even something more. Keep in mind that what organizations use, do, develop, and deliver to customers is evaluated on the basis of *both* customer satisfaction and usefulness of outputs.

Further, usefulness of what is delivered is based on sustained value and worth both to the client and to our shared world. Figure 3.1 shows the basic questions any organization asks and answers, whether it does so formally or not.

Conventional quality approaches focus on only one part of the mega/outcomes level: client satisfaction. Figure 1.5 (Chapter 1) showed the general rolling up of the typical quality management program elements. Notice that the sequence flows from quality resources ("because we have quality-driven suppliers, we don't have to inspect it; we know it's right") to processes ("everyone knows their jobs and assures it is done right") to results ("the product is right the first time and every time") that lead to client satisfaction.

The conventional QM vision, where we want to be, is focused at the output and the satisfied-customer levels. This level of results is vital. Let's look at the implications. Recall from Chapter 3 that the vision for a conventional QM effort in K-12 education might be as follows:

> To achieve total acceptance of the quality of education's graduates and completers; everyone will get a job or get accepted into a postsecondary accredited school; there will be no student who fails to graduate or complete a program. Clients' satisfaction will be indicated by surveys showing "good" or better judgments of the district's effectiveness.

Adding the Mega Level to QM: QM+

The vision of the typical QM effort is at the macro level— Question 2 of Figure 3.1—and/or is concerned with client satisfaction.

Of course, satisfied clients are crucial to a viable organization. But is that enough? Isn't there more? Let's see how to expand QM into *quality management plus* (QM+).

Comfort zones, paradigm shifts, and restructuring for educational success—revisiting our openness to change. Before moving ahead, we should realize that asking people to move out of their current paradigms and comfort zones—those boundaries and ground rules that they use to deal with everyday events and problems—can be greeted with fear, anger, and/or denial. As we first noted in Chapter 1, most people have learned how to deal with the realities and operations of today and they become edgy (or worse) when confronted with new realities.

Education, along with our entire world, has changed. We used to believe that there was a nuclear family, learners who came to school ready to learn and sporting their parents' encouragement to perform and succeed. We all know that world no longer exists (if it ever did at all). Quality management, as a process and way of thinking, chips away at "business as usual" and thus will invite resistance and perhaps denial.

We now might make matters even worse by opening the door to expand the scope of conventional QM. When we ask professionals (as well as parents and citizens) to move even beyond conventional (and vital) "quality management," be ready for sparks to fly. Asking anyone to give up their usual ways and understandings is to invite problems.

But we mortgage the future of our children and their children if we ignore the reality of a changed and changing world and the absolute vitality of

1. setting our objectives based upon a better future, not on improving today's efficiency;
2. using QM (and Joiner's three clusters of Deming's 14 points); and
3. extending QM to include defining and achieving the kind of world we want for tomorrow's child.

We must move ahead in this societally responsible mode, this QM extension we term *QM+*, with courage, conviction, and patience.

Quality Management "Plus" (QM+)

Beyond client satisfaction. Peter Drucker reminds us that doing things right is not as important as doing the right things. Quality management, as usually practiced, concentrates on doing things right.

But what about the contributions and usefulness of what satisfies the clients? We can think of many client-pleasing things that might not be helpful or even safe. A few items in the private sector that have resulted in client satisfaction (along with high sales and profits) that turned out to be unacceptable if not downright unhealthy include

- plastic bags (which are nonbiodegradable)
- Styrofoam cups/plastic packaging and utensils (which are nonbiodegradable)
- chemicals (DDT, Chlordane, Alar, blue food dye)
- well-marbled beef
- fried chicken with skin
- cigarettes/tobacco products
- disposable diapers
- newspaper ink (which is nonbiodegradable)
- aerosol/fluorocarbon sprays
- leaded gasoline
- asbestos insulation
- loud rock music/leaf blowers/horns
- suntans
- phosphates in washing detergents
- graduates (of programs for which there are no jobs)
- completers and graduates who go directly on welfare
- completers and graduates of programs who go to jail or mental institutions
- and so on

Quality usefulness. Each of the items (and you can probably add to the list) could be the subject of a QM process, and each would bring client satisfaction without (total) "quality usefulness" (to the client and our shared world). For example, we could be pleased with our graduating students only to realize later that they don't get jobs, they receive government support, and they often become social deviants. Farfetched? Research data indicate that most parents are happy with their own schools but feel that U.S. education is in serious trouble. Sound similar?

The missing quality consideration, what isn't explicit in standard QM, is delivering results that are good for society and that define and create an exemplary world. An ideal vision, in its most functional form, defines a shared vision of more than a successful school, a successful educational system, and/or a satisfied client. Nor should an ideal vision be simply an extrinsic vision intending to compete with another agency or organization (have the highest test score in the state, be the lowest in dropouts) but it should identify an ideal—even perfect—condition or world (Senge, 1990).

Taguchi's loss function (Taguchi & Phadke, 1984) is a step toward incorporating into QM the consequences of a system's actions on society. He defines quality to be the loss to society at the time of production of a good or service.

A practical and effective ideal vision defines a safe and satisfying world where everyone is self-sufficient, self-reliant, and mutually contributing (Kaufman, 1991; Kaufman & Herman, 1991). An ideal vision can and should provide the basis of deriving which part of that entire vision your educational agency will be responsible for providing. An illustration of how the organizational mission rolls down from the ideal vision is shown in Figure 4.1.

An "extended" QM—QM+—will link the ideal vision with conventional QM. It will add a complete mega level. QM+ will go beyond client satisfaction and include results that are useful in today's and tomorrow's worlds:

> All learners will complete and/or be certified, and there will be none who will not be self-sufficient, self-reliant, and have a self-judged acceptable quality of life (as indicated by their income being equal to or greater than their expenses and no suicide, commitment to mental institutions, or sentences to imprisonment for crimes).

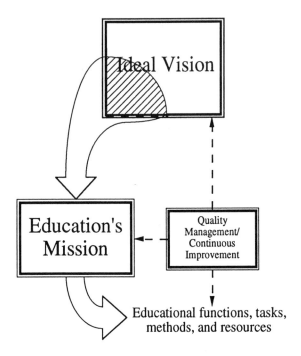

Figure 4.1. The Ideal Vision Provides the Basis for Determining What Education Will Contribute as a Part of the QM Process

Client satisfaction will be indicated by continued funding for the education system at or above the same levels (corrected for inflation).

Figure 4.2 provides a *quality management plus* (QM+) framework. The QM+ process begins outside the organization by identifying what is required for societal usefulness—or quality usefulness (the mega level again)—then rolling down to create what should be delivered to the client—if the mega vision is to be achieved—and then meeting with the roll-up contributions of conventional quality management. Quality management plus integrates with conventional quality management; it takes a good idea and extends it.

QM+ in education. A mega-level (or QM+) mission objective—based on the ideal vision—for a school system might be as follows:

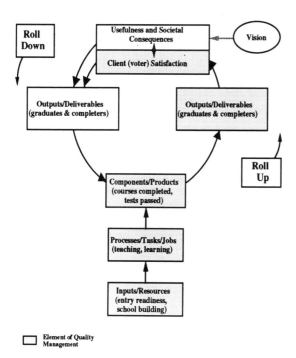

Figure 4.2. The Quality Management Plus Cycle
NOTE: Conventional quality management (QM) elements are shaded.
Note that the vision is focused on societal usefulness.

To achieve complete acceptance of the quality of education's graduates and completers as indicated by: everyone will get and keep a job (for at least 6 months) or get accepted into and complete a postsecondary accredited school; there will be no student who fails to graduate or complete and be self-sufficient and self-reliant and not under the care, custody, or control of another person, agency, or substance. As a result of this achievement and client satisfaction, the funding for education will continue so that there will be no new needs that develop that are not attended to within 1 year of identification.

To be sure, this is ideal. We might not get it achieved in our lifetime. But we owe it to ourselves and tomorrow's child to set our future direction based upon the ideal. We should not make ourselves self-limiting. When we restrict our vision to what we believe can be accomplished, our reach will be the same as our grasp, and we will forfeit any of our dreams.

These dreams, some might object, are not practical, not real world. There will be those that cry for us to be politically oriented and give up dreams, perhaps the same ones who derided Martin Luther King, Jr.'s "I have a dream" speech. They would likely sneer at Walt Disney's statement that if you can dream it you can do it.

The statement of a mega-level ideal vision and mission is real and practical. In fact, its absence from educational strategic planning (Kaufman, 1992b; Kaufman & Herman, 1991) is probably why many so-called educational innovations and change initiatives have not worked; they haven't been linked to current and future societal payoffs.

Aren't QM+ and the mega level all hypothetical and academic? Don't reject QM+ too quickly. Before deciding not to formally and specifically include societal well-being and added value as a rational extension of QM, consider some recent circumstances. First, how many companies in the *Fortune* 500 10 years ago are not there anymore? What about the Exxon Valdez, the old Ford Pinto, baby apple "juice," which turns out to be only flavored water? Would you want to be part of a company going into the cigarette business? Would you like to be heading up a new school district and announce at the outset that you are going to fail to graduate at least one third of all learners who come to school?

Delivering education that provides societal good is, increasingly, both possible and ethical. Some authors suggest that any organization that doesn't is self-limiting and will probably falter (Drucker, 1992; Kaufman, 1992a, 1992b; Senge, 1990).

What can I do? Educational planners and administrators are often the first to realize that something is missing from organizational missions, capabilities, and methods. They see the link between people, productivity, and organizational success but take a reactive posture and only attend to their piece of the puzzle.

When initiating a QM process, why not open a dialogue with all educational partners about going beyond the conventional QM framework by adding societal payoffs to client satisfaction? By deriving an ideal mega-level vision and adding that to the standard QM process, your educational system is likely to reap a richer harvest. If you do, you are likely to deliver both quality and demonstrate return on investment in societal terms to learners and taxpayers.

Doing a needs assessment for a QM+ *activity.* When doing QM+, the information from a conventional needs assessment (which usually only collects data up to the macro level) is augmented with the harvesting of the gaps in results at the full *mega* level, such as the additional ones shown in Table 4.1. Another variation of a needs assessment format that incorporates the mega level is provided in Table 4.2.

A needs assessment can (and we suggest should) deal with each level of possible quality: mega, macro, and micro. Basic questions that could be addressed in such a needs assessment are shown in Table 4.3. A checklist for a needs assessment is provided in Table 4.4.

The QM+ implementation process. Table 4.5 provides the 11 action steps (revised from a standard QM process) for implementing QM+. Recall that opportunities and maintaining what is already working should be considered at each step. We want the educational system to improve steadily without sacrificing in-place successful activities and resources.

What's to Be Gained by Using QM+?

Not only do organizations have to be competitive, they also must contribute to our future societal well-being. Futurists (see Naisbitt & Aburdene, 1990; Toffler, 1990) agree that a new world is coming our way, whether or not we are ready. For example, it will be a world where the knowledge-rich will prevail, where older distinctions

(Text continued on p. 105)

Table 4.1 Additional Mega-Level Variables, Such as These, May Be Added to the Needs Assessment Format Provided in Table 2.8 for an Educational Quality Management Plus Activity

	Current Results	Current Consequences	Desired Results	Desired Consequences
MEGA LEVEL				
Self-sufficient & self-reliant completers				
Sustained profits for private sector organizations				
Environmental state/condition				
Murder rate				
Health & well-being of completers				
Quality of life of completers				
Former students in who's who				
Image/reputation				
Board member satisfaction				
Employer satisfaction				
Etc...				
MACRO LEVEL				
Graduates/completers				
Licensures				
Accreditation				
Etc...				

Table 4.2 A Needs Assessment Summary Format That Includes the Mega Level

			Need Level			
Current Results	Possible Means	Desired Results	Ideal Vision	Micro	Macro	Mega

SOURCE: Kaufman (1992b).

103

Table 4.3 Questions to Be Asked and Answered in a Needs Assessment (and quasi-needs assessment)

TYPE OF NEEDS ASSESSMENT AND QUASI-NEEDS ASSESSMENT LEVELS		QUESTIONS TO BE ASKED AND ANSWERED
NEEDS: **Mega/Outcome**	#1	Am I concerned with closing the gaps in results related to the usefulness of that which my organization--school or district--delivers to our community and society?
Macro/Output	#2	Am I concerned with closing the gaps in results related to quality--meeting specifications for graduates and completers--of that which my organization delivers?
Micro/Product	#3	Am I concerned with closing the gaps in results related to the quality of that which an individual or a small group within my school or district produces (such as passing courses and tests)?
QUASI NEEDS: **Process**	#4	Am I concerned with the gaps in methods, techniques, and activities (such as curriculum, teaching methods) used?
Input	#5	Am I concerned with the gaps in availability and/or quality of resources used?

Table 4.4 A Needs Assessment Checklist

---

1. Does it target ends rather than means?
2. Does it cover the three levels of school of district concerns:
   - micro (products),
   - macro (outputs),
   - mega (outcomes)?
3. Is it free from assumptions concerning the solution (such as computers, in-service training, total quality management, site-based management, "excellence")?
4. Does it collect and use perception (soft) data about gaps in results from each of the three QM partner groups (recipients, implementors, and society/community)?
5. Does it collect and use performance-based results and not just the perceptions of the partners?
6. Does it identify the gaps in results in measurable performance terms?
7. Does it integrate the perception data with the performance data?
8. Does it place the gaps in priority order?
9. Does it provide the basis for changing where change is essential and continuing what's successful?

---

concerning rich and poor will have less importance. There will be an environment where knowledge—up-to-date and timely knowledge—truly is power. Conventional ways of viewing our world, and thus our current educational curricula, will not suffice.

To be responsive to that new reality, we must become active players in creating the kind of world (a) in which we want our children to live, (b) to which we can make a contribution, (c) from which we will get a return on our investment for what we do and deliver, and (d) for which we can (and will) be accountable for useful results.

By using a societal-payoffs dimension when setting our targets—moving beyond just client satisfaction to also include client and societal well-being—we can not only be responsive to our coming world, we can also be the masters of it. A happy client is not enough. One that continues to be a healthy, safe, *and* satisfied one is better.

It may be helpful for the quality partners to carefully and fully consider alternative levels that will be the formal and continuing concern of the process. Table 4.6 suggests possible QM focus statements. For each statement, the QM partners may negotiate their

Table 4.5 The QM+ Implementation Process

1. Define the ideal mega-level vision: the world in which we want tomorrow's child to live. Identify only results and conditions and do not include processes, resources, or methods. The extent to which the planning partners make this speak to results, not to favored initiatives or methods, is the degree to which this step will be useful.

2. Determine gaps between current conditions and the ideal vision.

3. Obtain agreement, based on the ideal vision, of the planning partners on what would deliver client satisfaction for future and closer-in years (year 2000, 1995, next year) and agree on how we would measure it. Identify the predicted needs—gaps in results—for each target year.

4. Define and specify the characteristics of the outputs of the educational system that would lead to clients' satisfaction and how we would measure it.

5. Define and specify the building-block results (mastery in courses, abilities, skills, knowledge, and so on) that would deliver what we identified in 1 and 2 above. Define how we would measure each.

6. Specify the activities (courses, initiatives, activities, and so on) that would deliver the building-block results, and what the specifications are for each.

7. Specify the resources—including people, facilities, funds, learner entry characteristics—required to deliver and complete the activities required to deliver the required results.

8. Specify what each person must do, continuously, to make certain that quality results and activities happen effectively and efficiently. Extend the quality system to include mega-level criteria and results that will be used by the QM team members.

9. Collect data on progress toward the ideal vision (defined in 1) and progress toward yearly objectives (in 3). Add mega-level variables and criteria to the possible variables already identified for QM. Possible variables to measure could include

absenteeism, course completions/failures/repeats, grades, test scores, truancy, dropouts, graduation rates, vocational occupational specialty certifications, criterion-referenced test results, standardized test results, job placements, counseling cases closed, audit exceptions, ethics violations, accidents, on-site fatalities, grievances, in-service training courses completed, certified competencies, sick leave, work samples.

When we use QM+, we might add mega-level variables, such as completed/noncompleted learners who are self-sufficient and self-reliant (not under the care, custody, or control of another person, agency, or substance); holding a job for a year or more; successful interpersonal relations (no/low divorce rate; no spouse/mate abuse, no successful harassment judgments against them, and so on); no felony convictions; quality of life in the community.

The exact criteria and variables to be part of the quality system should be determined by your QM team. In selecting variables to measure, be sure to identify indicators that will be an accurate and complete representation of all that education uses, does, accomplishes, and delivers as well as the societal and community payoffs.

10. Identify what educational activities and initiatives should be continued and which are to be revised to achieve useful quality.

11. Revise as required and continue what is working.

Table 4.6 A QM Agreement Table

	RESPONSE			
	Stake-holders		QM Planners	
	Y	N	Y	N
1. Each school, as well as the total educational system, will contribute to learners' current and future success, survival, health, and well-being.				
2. Each school, as well as the total educational system, will contribute to the learners' current and future quality of life.				
3. Learners' current and future survival, health, and well-being will be part of the system's and each of its schools' mission objectives.				
4. Each educational function will have objectives that contribute to 1, 2, and 3, above.				
5. Each job/task/activity will have objectives which contribute to 1, 2, 3, and 4, above.				
6. A Needs Assessment will identify and document any gaps in results at the operational levels of 1, 2, 3, 4, and 5, above.				
7. Educational learning requirements will be generated from the Needs identified and selected based on the results of 5.				
8. The results of 5 may recommend noneducational intervention(s).				
9. Evaluation will use data from comparing results with objectives for 1, 2, 3, 4, and 5.				

SOURCE: Based on Kaufman (1992b).

focus with key educational stakeholders and initial their agreement or disagreement with the statement.

Note that if any group declines to address any of the statements—is not willing to be on the same team—they assume the responsibility for the goal not being accomplished. Simply bringing up these possibilities in this way often clarifies the three levels of results and the importance of a QM+ focus.

When one uses QM+, changes (often dramatic) will be seen—and quickly. One difference might well be in the way curriculum, courses, and learning experiences are identified, designed, developed, and implemented and in how evaluation is used. Figure 4.3 provides a different curriculum (and learning experiences) framework.

Notice that educational curriculum and activities (not just courses)

are based upon current and future societal/community require-
    ments and opportunities;

are further based on skills, knowledge, attitudes, and abilities
    (SKAAs) required to deliver a better (or an ideal) society
    and community;

curriculum requirements are based on societal and community
    requirements and the detailed SKAAs;

learning opportunities (shown as "courses" in quotes to signify
    that alternative ways and means for delivering learning
    opportunities may be selected) are both identified and
    should be integrated to avoid the splintering of content and
    application;

learner entry SKAAs are used to determine learning opportuni-
    ties and pathways;

both existing and required resources are identified (and, because
    the payoffs will be clearly documented, new resources may
    be better justified in terms of costs to do the job right versus
    the costs for not delivering useful education);

learner performance is the basis for several types of revision:
    (a) Learners are certified as either completed or appropri-
    ate remediation is instituted and (b) the entire process may

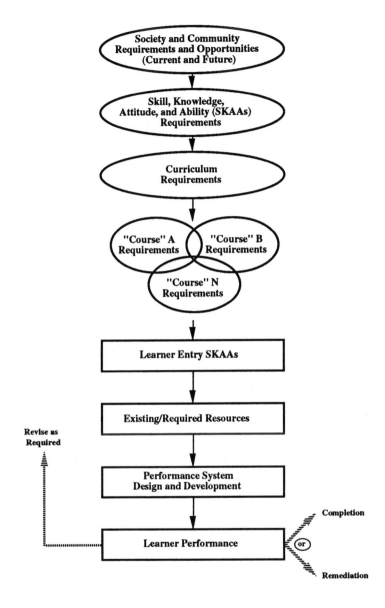

Figure 4.3. A Curriculum Development Process That Could Result
From Applying a Quality Management Plus Process
SOURCE: Kaufman (1992b).

be revised; the entire curriculum is a "learning and self-renewing" one, and what works and what doesn't is used to continuously improve it.

QM, QM+, Strategic Planning, Strategic Planning Plus (SP+), and Continuous Improvement

Continuous improvement of everything we do and deliver is a central concept in quality management as well as a primary focus of strategic planning. While we move closer and closer to our ideal vision, we assure improvement in every way every day. Continuous improvement should be occurring as a consequence of both QM and strategic planning. By adding an ideal vision and mega-level objectives to their core, there is an addition of growth and improvement to the mix.

Strategic planning, like QM, best includes societal and community payoffs and consequences, the mega level, or it may opt to limit itself to a lower results level (macro or micro). A strategic planning process, first shown in Figure 2.2, that allows a choice among results levels has been suggested by Kaufman (1992a, 1992b) and Kaufman and Herman (1991) and is shown in Figure 4.4.

Conventional (and useful but often self-limiting) strategic planning (see Cook, 1990; Kanter, 1989; Pfeiffer, Goodstein, & Nolan, 1989) approaches start below the mega level and use visions aimed at what is important for an organization itself to be successful. Visions developed in these approaches (if indeed they formally are) tend to be either macro level and/or competitive[1]—achieve the highest test scores in the state, win the teaching excellence award, or the like (Kaufman, 1992a, 1992b; Kaufman & Herman, 1991; Senge, 1990).

Strategic planning plus (SP+) (Kaufman, 1992a, 1992b; Kaufman & Herman, 1991) and QM+ add an ideal vision—defining the world in which we want tomorrow's child to live—and the dimension of mega-level planning. It should be emphasized that QM and classical strategic planning are not wrong, simply that they become more powerful when the mega-level concerns are added.

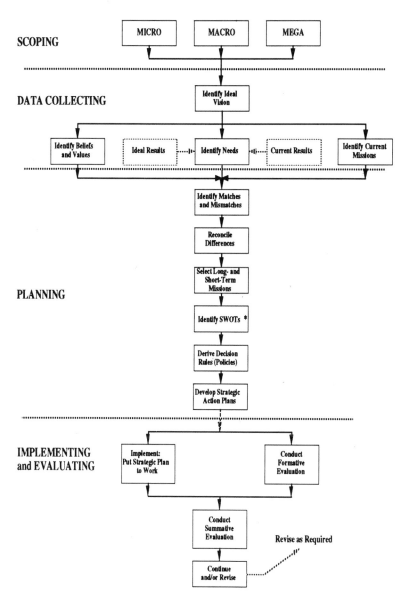

Figure 4.4. A Four-Level—Scoping, Data Collecting, Planning, and Implementation and Evaluation—Strategic Planning Process
SOURCE: Kaufman (1992b).
*Strengths, weaknesses, opportunities, and threats.

Our world has a global economy and a shared destiny, and simple appeals to be competitive again will not suffice. We have to define and create an ideal. We must develop leaders, thinkers, integrators, and contributors who can and will lead us there. To do this, we have to be creative, innovative, and inventive, for what must be done is not currently on the drawing boards. We have to add to our current models, techniques, and approaches that which will identify and create what will be required.

We Can Add the Plus Factor,
Even Without First Getting Permission

QM and QM+ are both a process and a way of thinking and acting. It makes sense to view education as a means to societal ends. Even if this concept is difficult for some of the QM partners, it doesn't have to stop you from simply adding it in as you do your work and participate in QM activities. If you add the plus factor into your QM work, very few will notice it. Arguments often come from a concern over whether or not mega-level data and agreement are possible, not from its rationality. (Of course, data are available. See, for example, Hintzen, 1990; Kaufman, 1992a, 1992b; Kaufman & Herman, 1991; MacGillis, Hintzen, & Kaufman, 1989; Sobel & Kaufman, 1989.) As most organizational practitioners realize, it is easier to beg forgiveness than it is to ask permission. By simply adding mega-level indicators to the QM specifications, most people won't notice, and those that do will probably thank you.

Our Ethical and Practical Choice

As educators, we have a choice. We can concentrate on process and resources—efficiency—and do what we are already doing at lower cost. Or we may define quality management to include the "plus" factor and define and create that which will be useful in today's and tomorrow's worlds. Toffler (1990) and Naisbitt and Aburdene (1990) are only three futurists demonstrating that our world has changed and that extending today's realities will once again leave us playing catch-up. If tomorrow's world is going to be closer to ideal than today's, education has to define new horizons and new ways to get from here to there.

The Boundaries for QM+

Ideally, the whole world should be the arena for QM+. As we move continuously closer toward that ideal, the question that every would-be improver of quality has to ask is this: "Where shall I start implementing QM+ in my system?"

The answer is anywhere you can. And move in both directions at once—as you achieve continuous improvement in your area, also expand into the areas around you. The bigger the area, the more likely your success:

better the national educational system than the state;

better the state educational system than the district;

better the district than the school;

better the school than the class;

better the class than the individual teacher;

better the individual teacher than not starting at all.

For a change, bigger is better, as long as you get everyone committed—really committed—to continuous improvement of education.

Figure 4.5 shows relationships among the various QM+ activities for a site-based continuous improvement process. Whether we realize it or like it or not, all levels are linked and are sensitive to each other.

Quality is an infectious thing. Some people might be simply waiting in the wings to see how well you do. With your success, they might be willing to join you in a larger arena. Start your quality initiative anywhere you can and get everyone in the system—those around you—to have a passion for quality, with all of you being on the same team, committed to making data-based decisions using valid, reliable, and unbiased data.

Note

1. Or, these could be called, in Senge's (1990) terms, extrinsic.

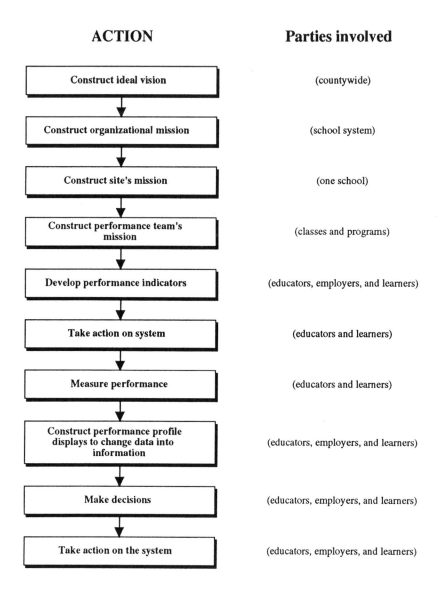

Figure 4.5. An Example of a Site-Based Continuous Improvement Process

The Quality System

Assuring Scientific Bases for Decision Making

The Importance of High Quality Data in Decision Making

The Quality System as a
Vital Part of QM and QM+

Balance. Again: A passion for quality is not enough. Everyone on one team is not enough. Data-based decisions are not enough. QM success depends upon balance among passion, teamwork, and useful data.

The data base is the management and control "heart" of a QM system. A quality system—the collection and use of performance data to

115

assure progress and useful results—is the "scientific" component of the QM process. Continuous progress toward the (ideal) vision depends upon management and control of the educational processes and contributions. Data, high quality data, are critical. Without useful and timely statistics, rational decisions cannot be made. If members of an educational enterprise intend to achieve quality, the quality team must know what's working and what isn't so they can revise as required.

We won't be providing lengthy discussions about statistics, quality control, quality improvement, or information displays. We will describe the processes involved in collecting reliable and valid data on a system and analyzing the data to provide accurate information. That information will be a basis for taking action on the system to achieve continuous improvement. The emphasis in this chapter will be on describing straightforward statistical tools. We will identify the assumptions being made when using these tools and the risks—there always are—being taken. We will identify resources that explain how to address more complex statistical issues that might arise when doing QM+.

Partnerships and the use of statistics in QM+. The process for systematically improving quality includes commitments to quality, to teamwork, and to data-based decisions. All partners must continually search for information that will allow everyone to continuously improve the quality of the results of their processes. Without the data base that a quality system provides, partners won't know how they are progressing or what to do next: There will be no basis for data-based decisions.

Timely data must be collected on critical success factors of the processes. The data must be summarized in a form that provides useful information to the decision makers. This will allow them to make decisions, take action on the system, and move toward the vision while systematically improving the quality of the enterprise. Figure 5.1 displays this process.

Statistics: Use for improving, never for blaming. Use of data for anything other than improving the system contradicts the values

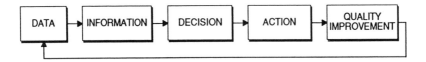

Figure 5.1. The Process Linking Data Collection and Quality Improvement

of QM+. Many of us have had negative experiences with data gathered for evaluation: It has rarely been a process that enhanced our well-being and showed us opportunities for constructive action. Usually it involved assessment of what went wrong, who was to blame, and what must change so that this won't go wrong in the future.

Given these negative experiences with evaluation, many of us carry a substantial amount of "evaluation anxiety." Hence any talk of rigorously gathering data to improve the quality of a system is likely to elicit evaluation anxiety from the partners. This produces resistance to rigorously gathering data on the system. Adding to the anxiety is the fact that most people—perhaps 90%—have had bad experiences when taking undergraduate statistics. In this chapter, we hope to make up for those earlier discomforting activities.

An essential step to take before gathering data is to ensure that empowering relationships—in which authority and responsibility have been turned over to the partners—have been created within the organization. A critical part of empowering relationships is the confidence that the different partners have that everyone will be honest with each other, will not make them wrong, and is aligned on the same goals. It is critical that individuals not do quality improvement activities while fearing that the data to be gathered will be used to punish them in some way.

QM+ is a caring approach to education. We care enough about learners, citizens, and our shared world to provide students with useful skills, knowledge, attitudes, and abilities to be successful in school and life, to help them create a better world.

High quality data provide the basis for a "structured caring"—caring enough about all educational partners, including learners, to precisely identify progress and problems. The quality system must be designed and used in a way that will provide high quality data that will deliver a "structured caring."

Rigor in the collection and use of data is perhaps best assured by collecting data that answer questions that are important to at least one of the partners. Data will be most useful if they relate to the questions posed in Table 2.3. Ends and means are to be related and data collected to assess how effectively the means employed are producing the ends desired. Needs must be defined and reported in terms of gaps in results (not gaps in inputs or processes).

There are always more potential questions on which to gather data than anyone could physically accomplish pursuing. Even if all the questions could be studied, the mountain of data would be more than the resources available to analyze and use them. Thus selectivity in the choice of what to measure is essential. Measure the questions that will produce the data that will give you the greatest openings for reaching your objectives and meeting needs.

This principle is illustrated in the experience of a restaurant seeking to assess customer satisfaction. The management explored one potential indicator of customer satisfaction after another with no success. Finally, someone suggested using tips as an indicator. This proved to be an excellent indicator and created numerous openings for action. Waitresses with unusually high tips were studied by other waitresses so as to improve themselves. When tips were uniformly high or low for the entire wait staff, successes or breakdowns in the kitchen were often the cause.

Continuous improvement then is the only use of data produced by the quality system. Data will help us decide what to keep, what to change, and what to stop. Data can be developed to make decisions on what is working and what isn't to more effectively take action on the system. The quality system will allow us to monitor, in an ongoing manner, improvement that is being made on the basis of changes instituted. We will be able to observe trends that are occurring in the system and summarize them in a form that is understandable and that empowers the partners to see additional openings for action.

Decisions and Continuous Improvement:
Getting the Facts

Basic Statistical Tools:
The Study of Populations

Toward this end, we will first present a description of basic statistical tools in the most straightforward settings in which they are useful in QM+. These applications will involve uses of statistical tools to study static populations by sampling and measuring them at one point in time.

We'll then move to a richer set of statistical applications that study processes that are producing results as time passes. Data are gathered by sampling the results over time. The data are analyzed to indicate what action will be advantageous on the sampled process.

The bad news (up until now) for an educational partner who has decided to implement quality management and for whom statistics has been a unpleasant part of his or her past is that the implementation of QM+ requires extensive use of straightforward statistical concepts and tools. Steps 2, 6, 9, 10, and 11 of the QM+ implementation process (Table 4.5) can be sensibly done only with extensive use of basic statistics.

The good news is that these statistical concepts and tools do not require an advanced degree in statistics to master them. In fact, motivated high school-educated production workers can master and use what we describe—once they get beyond the "statistics are scary" paradigm.

Simply, data tell us what's happened and what hasn't. We show you how to collect and use quality data to fix what has not worked and continue what has made a contribution. On our way to this, we will talk about sampling—getting snapshots of reality—and how to make sense out of data. There are a number of ways to display your results so that data can help you improve—continuously. First, let's talk about what data to gather and from whom.

The study of a population. To do Step 2 of the QM+ implementation process, in which one determines gaps between current conditions and the ideal vision, one must first identify the population that one is considering. For example, with a high school, the *population* of interest may be all students who graduated last year. The *variable* of interest—that is, the characteristic, the quality, or the aspect of each graduate—may be the status of the graduate: whether or not he or she is employed or has moved on to higher education. Another variable is his or her score on a *hypothetical* Life Skills Management Test (LSMT) consisting of 30 questions.

Now, suppose that, for each of these variables, the educational partners have agreed on a vision, perhaps derived from an ideal vision, in which all learners are self-sufficient and self-reliant or are progressing toward being so:

- Within 6 months after graduation,

    - 100% of the high school graduates will be either employed or in higher educational institutions and

    - at least 90% will score at least 27 out of 30 on the Life Skills Management Test.

To determine the gaps between the current results and the vision, we must measure individuals in last year's graduating class on these two variables. Let us assume that the school we are studying is sizable, with a graduating class of 600. Measurement of all 600 would involve resources that are not available to the QM+ project. So, we are in a situation where sampling is required.

As another example, suppose our ideal vision included that "all learners will be self-sufficient economically within 6 months after graduation or leaving or be at least three fourths time enrolled in a college or university." What might our needs assessment data look like? A sample of 145 students might yield the information summarized in Table 5.1. Therefore, for these data, our gap in results— need—is between 98 and 145, or 32% of our sample are not achieving the desired results.

Sampling. The sampling process is an essential part of a statistical investigation. To return to our original example, if we draw a random sample of 50 students from the 600 who graduated last year and then

Table 5.1 Distribution of Graduates and Leavers According to Our (partial) Ideal Vision

	Earnings ≥ Expenses	Earnings < Expenses	≥ ¾ in Higher Education	< ¾ in Higher Education	Sum
Graduates 1991	37	7	40	16	100
Leavers 1991	21	22	0	2	45
Sum	58	29	40	18	145

Meeting Ideal Criteria	Not Meeting Ideal Criteria
98(58 + 40)	47(29 + 18)

measure each individual sampled on our two variables, *status* and *LSMT score*, we will be able to make some powerful statements about the population of students and their status relative to employment, higher education, and the Life Skills Management Test.

Suppose we select this random sample and do the measurements and the calculations properly. From our sample of 50 students, we will determine the sample proportion of students who are employed 6 months after high school graduation or are in higher education. This will be an "unbiased estimate" of the proportion of the population of students who are employed or in higher education. By "unbiased," we mean that the estimate (the proportion we get from the sample) will be, on average, equal to the proportion we would have obtained had we interviewed the entire population of 600 students. The proportion of students in the population employed or going on to higher education is a *parameter* of our population of values. For example, if 360 students had a job or went on to higher education, the parameter (the population proportion) would equal $p = 360/600 = .60$.

The proportion we determine from our sample is called a *statistic*: a number that can be computed from the data in our sample. It is the sample proportion of students going on to higher education. If 35 of the students in the sample went on to higher education, the statistic (the sample proportion) would be $\hat{p} = 35/50 = .70$. The statistic $\hat{p}$ is an estimate of the parameter p.

Other sampling tactics. But we have gotten ahead of ourselves in the statistical process involved in doing this study. There are other sampling strategies that can be used in this situation. For example, if one wishes to ensure that the sample in the needs assessment study exactly reflects the gender and racial composition of the graduating class as a whole, one can select a *stratified sample* in which the 600 students are first (using school records) divided into groups by gender and race.

For example, there may be five racial categories, African American/black, white, hispanic, Asian, and other, which combine with the two genders to produce 10 different groups of students in the graduating class. Then, we could draw a random sample from each one of those 10 groups, determine sample proportions of students in higher education for each of the 10 groups, and use statistical formulas to combine these 10 different estimates into one overall estimate of the population proportion of students in that high school going on to higher education.

A description of the nuts and bolts of doing simple random sampling can be found in most introductory statistics books (e.g., Weiers, 1991, chap. 6). Descriptions of stratified sampling and the formulas that are necessary to implement it can be found in Schaeffer, Mendenhall, and Ott (1990).

Measurement. Once the sampling process has been done effectively, the next activity is to measure the subjects—the learners selected. Keep in mind that the measurement process is as essential to the production of high quality data as is the sampling process. The measurement process involves assigning a number to each one of our selected learners that reflects his or her score on the variable we are interested in measuring. Thus we may record a "1" if the student says "Yes," she is either employed or in an institution of higher education, and a "0" if she is not. The score on the LSMT may be the number of questions that the student answered correctly.

Operational definitions. An *operational definition* is a set of procedures that can be applied to a subject to provide a score on a variable that is specific enough so that different observers using the definition would arrive at the same (or nearly the same) score. To operationally define something is to define it in terms of how we measure it.

For example, we talk about "good district management" but really "operationally define" it by how we judge it: teacher and staff turnover, superintendent tenure, community financial support over time, and so on. For another example, in asking a student whether he or she is employed or in higher education, key issues to be addressed include the following:

- What do we mean by "employed"? Is it full-time employment? Is it part-time employment? Is it employment at or above a certain salary?
- What about "involved in higher education"? What does that mean? Does going to a technical school count? How about a community college? Does the person have to be enrolled full time? What about people who are half-time university students and half-time employees? Do they count as being in this group?

After consideration of issues such as these, the educational partner doing the needs assessment may, for example, develop an operational definition in this situation that addresses the above concerns as follows:

- Individuals will be regarded as employed or in an institution of higher education if
  - they are either employed for at least 30 hours per week, or
  - they are full-time students at a post-high school technical school, community college, or university, or
  - they are employed some fraction of full time and are enrolled at some fraction of a full-time load, where the two fractions combine to at least three quarters.

There are similar issues relating to what we mean by the LSMT score of a student:

- What test will be used to measure this? What questions will be on the exam? Is the test valid? Reliable? How long will the students have to complete the exam? What resources will be available to them: calculator, dictionary, encyclopedia, telephone?

Reliability, bias, and validity. The purpose in developing precise operational definitions is to allow the educational partners to collect reliable data. Data are *reliable* if repeated observations of the same subject would produce the same (or virtually the same) score. Operational definitions also allow the collection of unbiased data. The measurement process is *unbiased* if repeated measurements of the same subject, on average, give the "true value" for that subject. An extended discussion of these concepts is given by Moore (1991).

An example of an unbiased measurement process can be seen in considering an object weighed on a scale. If the object is certified by the National Bureau of Standards to weigh 10 grams and if repeated weighing of the object on the scales produce measurements whose average is 10 grams, then that measurement process is said to be unbiased. The reliability of that measurement process is assessed by how close together the repeated measurements of the weight are. The closer together these measurements are, the more reliable is the measurement process.

Another important aspect of the measurement process is *validity.* A variable is said to be a valid measure of a particular property if it is an accurate and appropriate reflection of that property: if it measures what it says it measures. For example, using height to measure leadership is an example of an invalid measurement. Height is not accurate or appropriate as a measure of leadership. Using height as a measure (or indicator) of one's physical stature, however, is an example of a valid measure.

Suppose that five experts on life skills management issues examined the Life Skills Management Test we plan to use in our needs assessment. If all five agreed that the questions asked are germane to life skills management, then the test would have *content validity.*

Other variables, such as whether individuals are employed or in higher education, appear to be valid measures of the phenomena we want them to reflect. Measures like this are said to have *face validity* because they seem to be related to what they are measuring.

"Valid indicators" sometimes aren't. In certain areas of educational assessment, validity issues are difficult and critical. One of these is the issue of accountability. The response to a legislative requirement that school systems produce statistics that measure their productivity and how well they are responding to mandates of accountability sometimes produces studies reflecting the number of students per classroom or the number of students graduating or the number of students who are participating in various programs.

Whether these variables are valid measures of a school's productivity is questionable. They count certain characteristics of the school's performance to be sure. A variable, such as the number of students who graduate, however, does not reflect whether the students who graduate are capable of finding and keeping a job or getting into an institution of higher learning. A key issue in resolving validity issues is to carefully develop operational definitions for the constructs to be measured in an assessment of accountability. For a further discussion of validity, see Moore (1991).

Collecting useful data. Another aspect of the measurement process is the method by which information is obtained. Will data be gathered by face-to-face interviews, written test, performance samples, telephone interviews, or mailed questionnaires? What are the advantages and disadvantages of each of these methods in terms of the cost of the data collection and the quality of the resulting data? An extensive discussion of these topics as well as meticulous guidance in how to do effective mail and telephone surveys is provided in Dillman (1978).

Applying the measurement process to the subjects selected in the sampling process produces the *sample of values.* This can be represented as a matrix. In our hypothetical study, suppose that we have measured 50 students on two variables using a mailed questionnaire. The sample of values matrix would be a 50×2 matrix, where the rows represent the individual students in our study and the columns represent the two variables being measured on those students. Let us assume that our study yielded the sample of values given in the last two columns of Table 5.2. Figure 5.2 represents the different parts of the study of a population that we have been discussing.

Though the sample of values matrix contains all the data gathered, it is too cumbersome to provide information on which to make data-based decisions and then take action on our educational process. Fortunately, many procedures have been developed to summarize the data so that its message will be clear and understandable.

Descriptive statistics. The descriptive statistics process is the set of steps employed to extract information from the sample values. This process yields a description of the individuals on variables included in the sample as well as the behavior of relationships between pairs of variables, triples of variables, and so on. A guiding principle in the descriptive statistics process is that the description produced (whether graphic or numerical) will be an accurate reflection of the data in the entire sample of values.

Useful information should not be lost or obscured by the process of describing the data. We can display it so it makes sense even to non-data-oriented people. In the following pages, we will show you a number of display possibilities:

- sequence plots
- bar charts
- side-by-side histograms
- scattergrams
- cause-and-effect diagrams
- control charts
- histograms
- pie charts
- stacked bar histograms
- Pareto diagrams
- flowcharts

And we will give applied examples of each and suggest when each might be best used.

Table 5.2 The Sample of Values

LEARNER NUMBER	STATUS Response	Code	LIFE SKILLS MANAGEMENT TEST SCORE
1	NO	0	18
2	NO	0	2
3	YES	1	21
4	YES	1	29
5	YES	1	27
6	YES	1	23
7	YES	1	22
8	YES	1	30
9	NO	0	4
10	NO	0	16
11	NO	0	3
12	NO	0	20
13	NO	0	9
14	YES	1	21
15	YES	1	17
16	YES	1	30
17	YES	1	24
18	YES	1	30
19	YES	1	27
20	YES	1	28
21	YES	1	25
22	YES	1	26
23	NO	0	10
24	YES	1	22
25	YES	1	15
26	YES	1	15
27	YES	1	21
28	YES	1	26
29	NO	0	12
30	YES	1	30
31	NO	0	7
32	YES	1	30
33	YES	1	18
34	YES	1	30
35	NO	0	5
36	NO	0	25
37	YES	1	23
38	YES	1	21
39	YES	1	29
40	YES	1	27
41	YES	1	19
42	YES	1	24
43	NO	0	13
44	YES	1	24
45	NO	0	25
46	YES	1	11
47	YES	1	23
48	NO	0	14
49	YES	1	23
50	YES	1	26

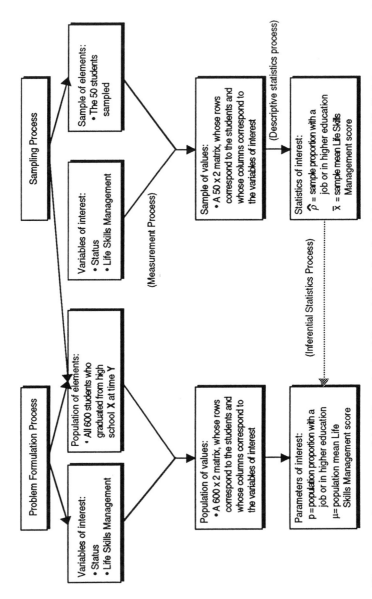

Figure 5.2. Summary of the Hypothetical Population Study of Status and Life Skills Management Test (LSMT) Scores

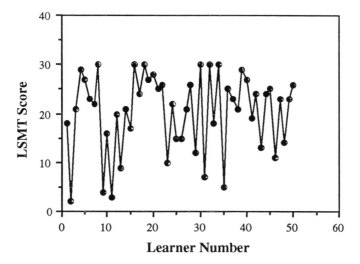

Figure 5.3. Sequence Plot of LSMT Scores With No Order Effect (Case 1)

Data displays for making decisions. A first step to ensure that the descriptive statistics principle is being followed is to plot the data in the order in which they were measured (if, in fact, they were not all measured at the same time). This plot is called a *sequence plot.* In it, the sequence number of the observation is plotted along the horizontal axis while the actual value of the observation is plotted along the vertical axis. The sequence number reflects the order in which the responses were received. Figure 5.3 gives a sequence plot of the LSMT scores for the 50 students in our sample.

Figure 5.3 indicates that the observations are being measured with no apparent order effect. The sequence appears to be random, without any apparent trends or aberrant observations. (The description of control charts below will give us formal statistical tools to verify that our visual interpretation of this plot is accurate.) In this situation, no useful information will be lost by collapsing the data and computing the histogram for LSMT scores given in Figure 5.4.

This histogram indicates that the overall distribution of LSMT scores is skewed to the left, with the modal histogram interval, that

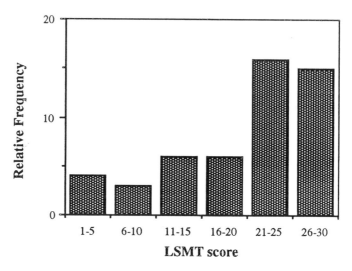

Figure 5.4. Histogram of the (LSMT) Scores

is, the interval containing the most observations being the one centered at 23, which contains scores from 21 to 25, inclusive.

Figure 5.5 shows another way in which these data could have
occurred. If order were important, then the LSMT scores might be
dropping for the measurements gathered later in the sample, as is
shown. This suggests that the individuals with stronger life management skills responded earlier, with the scores decreasing as time
passed. Suppose now that 75 questionnaires were mailed out and
that 50 were returned. Figure 5.5 leads us to expect that the subjects
who did not respond at all may be the ones with the weakest LSMT
scores.

We would be making a potentially serious error if we assumed
that the average LSMT score seen in the sample of 50 respondents
accurately reflects what would be seen if we had also gathered data
from the 25 nonrespondents. The data in Figure 5.5 produce the same
histogram as was produced for the data in Figure 5.3. Hence we
would also be making an error to assume that the LSMT score
distribution seen in the 50 respondents reflects the distribution of
LSMT scores in the 25 nonrespondents.

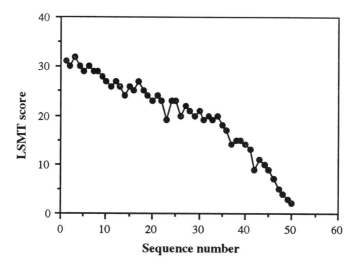

Figure 5.5. Sequence Plot of LSMT Scores With an Order Effect (Case 2)

Tactics. We suggest a sequence plot be done for each of the variables in the data set whose information was gathered in a time sequence before any further analyses are done. Those variables for which sequence effects are present are identified by extensive runs up or down in the sequence plot or by other distinctive nonrandom patterns. They should be set aside for future separate consideration.

More graphic descriptive statistics. Additional graphic descriptive statistics can be organized by the number of the variables being examined—1, 2, 3, or more—and the level of measurement of each variable. Kaufman (1992a) identifies four scales of measurement:

Nominal: naming something (for instance, "excellence," "fun," "Jan," "productivity")

Ordinal: Defining things as greater than, equal to, or less than other things (for instance, "Productivity is higher this month", "This pastoral painting is better than the portrait, and both are better than the still life over there.")

Interval: Relating items along a scale beginning at an arbitrary zero point and divided into equal intervals (for instance, temperature in degrees Celsius or IQ as measured by WISC)

Ratio: Relating items along a scale beginning at a known zero point and divided into equal intervals (for instance, temperature in degrees Kelvin, weight, distance, annual income)

As noted in Chapter 3, a mission statement is an intent that is measurable on a *nominal* or *ordinal* scale. A mission objective adds precise criteria to the mission statement and is measurable on an *interval* or *ratio* scale.

Suppose that the variable measured is at the interval or ratio level. For such a variable, the numbers measured for the values of the variable on learners in the sample actually have meaning as numbers, as representations of a quantity. Such is the case with LSMT scores, where the values on this variable represent the number of items correct on the LSMT. In this case, the histogram is usually employed to illustrate the distribution of scores seen for the variable in the sample. An example was presented in Figure 5.4.

If a variable, on the other hand, is measured at the nominal or ordinal level—as is our variable: "Is the graduate employed or in higher education?"—the statistical tool used to summarize that information is a *bar chart*, if the sequence plot indicates that the process that produced the data is stable over time. *Pie charts* depict this information in a circle graph that is divided into several pieces, similar to pieces of pie, where the size of each piece is proportional to the percentage of the learners in each category. Pie charts are not recommended for describing these data, because they make it difficult to compare the fraction of the sample in different segments of the pie. We prefer to use bar charts to represent the relative frequency of the different categories.

To illustrate this point, we have refined our nominal-level variable so that it now has four values: "employed only" *or* "in higher education only" *or* "both employed and in higher education" *or* "neither employed nor in higher education." Figures 5.6 and 5.7

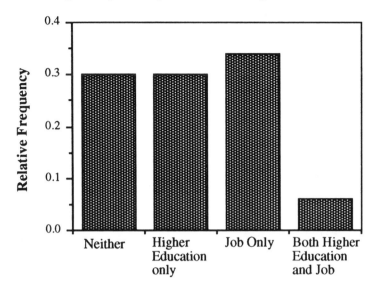

Figure 5.6. Bar Chart for Current Status of Respondents

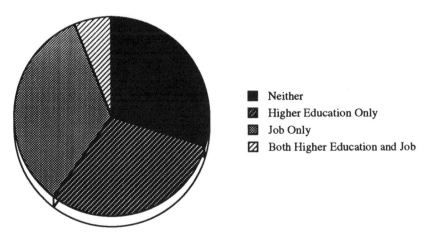

Figure 5.7. Pie Chart for Current Status of Graduates

show that comparisons of the relative frequency of the different responses in the pie chart are more difficult to make with confidence than are similar comparisons in the bar chart.

These figures reveal that slightly more than 30% of the graduates have a job only; 30% neither have a job nor are enrolled in higher education; 30% are enrolled in higher education; and about 5% are enrolled in higher education and have a job.

Two-variable analyses. The histogram for the LSMT data, as presented in Figure 5.4, gives the result of looking only at one variable, the LSMT score, and ignoring all other characteristics of the students that may have some impact on or relation to the LSMT score. Thus, if we interpret this graph as a representation of the LSMT score distribution in our entire population, we are assuming that this distribution is the same distribution that is seen in all subsets of our population of high school students: males versus females, African American/black versus white versus Hispanic versus other; students from single parent homes versus students from two parent homes; and so on.

To investigate whether this assumption is valid, we must examine two variables at a time. This analysis then opens up the questions: How do these two variables relate? Is there any apparent connection between the two? Does the distribution of one change when we consider different values of the other? There are three situations that may arise here: two interval- or ratio-level variables, one interval- or ratio-level variable and one nominal- or ordinal-level variable, and two nominal- or ordinal-level variables.

When examining the relationship between two nominal- or ordinal-level variables, the usual display is a *two-way contingency table*, which reflects the number of subjects in each category defined by the different levels of the two variables under consideration. Table 5.3 is an example of a two-way contingency table showing the relation of gender and status with respect to employment and higher education.

When one variable is nominal or ordinal level and the other is interval or ratio level, there are other possibilities: *side-by-side histograms* and *stacked bar histograms*. These are represented in Figures 5.8 and 5.9, respectively. The side-by-side histogram has advantages

Table 5.3 The Sample of 50 Respondents, Classified by Gender and Status

GENDER	NEITHER	HIGHER EDUCATION ONLY	JOB ONLY	BOTH HIGHER EDUCATION AND JOB	TOTALS
Male	10	7	5	1	23
Female	5	8	12	2	27
TOTALS	15	15	17	3	50

because of the ease with which one can compare the relative frequencies of the different categories to see how the distribution of LSMT scores varies depending on one's status.

These figures show that the LSMT scores for the respondents in higher education or having a job tend to be larger than for the respondents who neither are in higher education nor have a job.

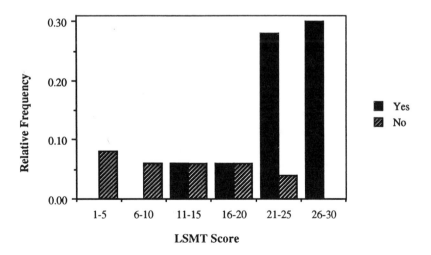

Figure 5.8. Side-by-Side Histogram for LSMT by Status

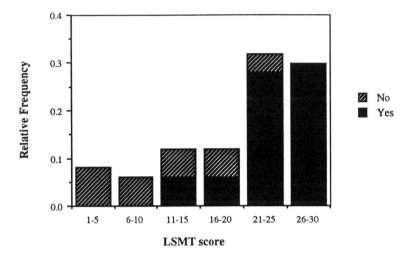

Figure 5.9. Stacked Bar Histogram for LSMT by Status

When comparing two interval- or ratio-level variables, the traditional tool to use is a *scattergram*. An example of this is found in Figure 5.10, where we have pictured the relationship between LSMT score and the student's GPA in high school. This figure shows that there is a positive association between LSMT and GPA, with higher LSMT scores occurring with higher GPAs and vice versa.

Each of the previous three graphs allows an education partner to discover if there is any apparent relationship between one variable, such as LSMT, and another variable. Presenting two-variable relationships such as these, as though they were true in all circumstances, involves making another assumption: The two-variable relationship is the same across all levels of all possible third variables. For example, ignoring gender when reporting the apparent relationship between LSMT scores and high school GPA is based on the assumption that the relationship between LSMT and GPA is the same for males and females. The only way to check this is to bring possibly important third variables, such as gender, into the analysis.

We can plot the LSMT versus GPA data separately for the males and the females to see if the resulting graphs have the same shape.

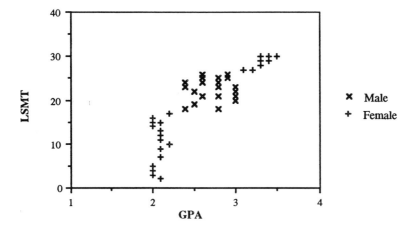

Figure 5.10. Scattergram of LSMT versus GPA

Unfortunately, it is possible for the overall relationship between LSMT and GPA to be markedly different than the relationship between these two variables, for males and females separately, as is seen in Figures 5.11 and 5.12. Notice that these two scattergrams show a *positive* relationship between LSMT and GPA for females and *no relationship* between LSMT and GPA for males.

So, there is always a danger whenever one presents a histogram, or a scatterplot, or even a scatterplot with separate plots for males and females: These one-, two-, and three-variable analyses can only reflect the variables in the analyses. There may be subsets of subjects defined by some other variable in which the pattern of responses for the current variables is much different than for the group as a whole. For example, the pattern observed may vary depending on neighborhood or number of children in the family.

There is an unending tension between the risks of ignoring additional variables and asserting that the graphs currently drawn represent an accurate picture of the relationships among these variables. There could be unseen differences embedded in different parts of the population. But, is it worth the cost of continuing to explore more and more variables with the resulting costs of delaying completion of the analysis and the project and of increasing the

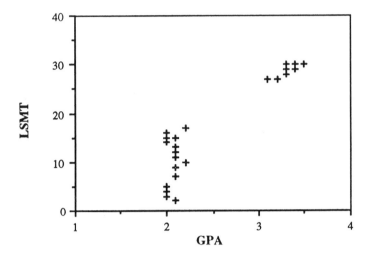

Figure 5.11. Scattergram of LSMT Versus GPA for Females

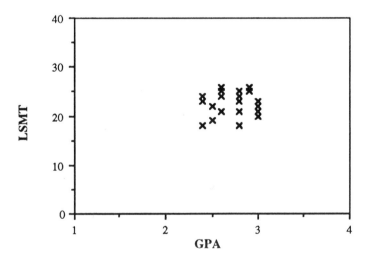

Figure 5.12. Scattergram of LSMT Versus GPA for Males

complexity of the analysis? In our experience, a useful tactic is to consult with individuals experienced in the field of inquiry. Ask about what variables in previous studies have been found to relate to one another or to modify relationships between other variables. You might ask, "What might I find out if I probe further—and what could I find that would significantly affect the learners' futures? Is it worth it?"

Numerical descriptive statistics. Graphic descriptive statistics are informative; they are also space consuming. There is value in developing more succinct summaries of the data, that is, numerical descriptive statistics. The most widely used of these give measures of the location of the data, that is, the average magnitude of the data and the variability of the data: how spread out the observations are from one another. The usual measures of location (or central tendency) are the *mean, median,* or *mode,* while the usual measures of spread are the *standard deviation* and the *range.* These numerical descriptive statistics and their advantages and disadvantages are discussed in introductory statistics books, such as Weiers (1991).[1] Figures 5.13 and 5.14 present information about the measures of location and spread, respectively.

The Study of Process

To execute Steps 9, 10, and 11 of the 11 action steps for implementing QM+, one must monitor a process, a sequence of steps for producing a result, over time. On the basis of the data collected over time, one must decide what action to take on that process. Unfortunately, the studies of populations described in the previous section are not adequate for this purpose. We must go a bit deeper.

As an example of a study of a process, let's suppose that we are interested in studying the number of in-school detentions per week as a measure of the quality of the learning environment in a particular school. We have decided that a valid indicator of a learning environment is the number of in-school detentions. The micro-level objectives include the condition of no in-school detentions, and thus none of the disruptions to the learning environment that occur when an incident arises that produces an in-school detention.

Mean = Arithmetic average of all the
observations = $\bar{x}$

Median = Value having the property that
half the observations are greater
and half are less than this value

Mode = Most frequently occurring value
in the data set

Figure 5.13. Measures of location (or central tendency).

Here we are studying a process, the sequence of steps involved in assigning a student to in-school detention. To see how well this process is functioning, we must follow it over time and collect data on the indicators that we deem useful as measures of the process.

Suppose that we have gathered data over the past 25 weeks on the number of in-school detentions per week at this particular school. The data are displayed in Table 5.4. The questions that the administrator is examining here are these: "What can be predicted for the in-school detention rate next week? How is this process behaving? Are the data implying that this problem is getting more severe so that we should change the system?"

Figure 5.15 represents a histogram of the data in Table 5.4. From that histogram, we see that the distribution is skewed to the right, with a median of 7. Using population study tools to assess the behavior of a process misses essential pieces of information. For

Range = Largest observation – Smallest observation

Variance = $$\frac{\sum_{i=1}^{n} (x_i - \bar{x})^2}{n - 1} = s^2,$$ where x_i denotes an individual score and $\bar{x}$ denotes the sample mean

Standard Deviation = $\sqrt{s^2} = s$

Figure 5.14. Measures of spread

Table 5.4 In-School Detention Counts, by Week

WEEK	Number of in-school detentions
1	15
2	10
3	3
4	9
5	9
6	6
7	7
8	8
9	5
10	3
11	9
12	6
13	8
14	4
15	8
16	15
17	8
18	6
19	5
20	3
21	8
22	5
23	3
24	4
25	8
(INTERVENTION)	
26	7
27	6
28	4
29	5
30	4
31	4
32	3
33	2
34	4
35	1

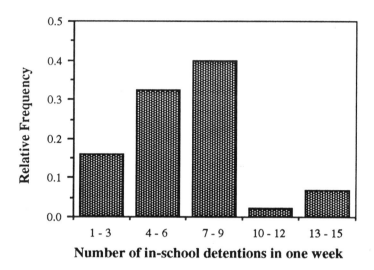

Figure 5.15. Histogram of Detention Results for 25 Weeks

example, Figures 5.16, 5.17, and 5.18 represent three different ways in which this process may be behaving and still produce the counts given in Table 5.4 and the histogram given in Figure 5.15.

Figure 5.16 indicates a process that is stable in which the variation about the median of 7 is random and unpredictable. Figure 5.17 depicts a situation in which the in-school detention rate started out very high but then reduced steadily over the 25 weeks till it is close to zero at the end of the period. Figure 5.18 represents the opposite of Figure 5.17.

Each of Figures 5.16 to 5.18 represents a situation that would produce different predictions for the next week and would also produce different actions relative to the in-school detention system. Thus making decisions about processes on the basis of cross-sectional or population-type tools, such as a histogram, may be very misleading.

So, what tools can be used to improve the quality of a process? The first step in studying any process is to construct a *process flowchart* of the steps in the process from beginning to end. This step almost invariably surfaces disagreements among the team members as to

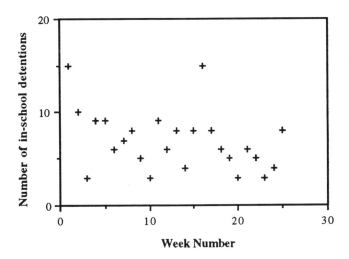

Figure 5.16. Sequence Plot of Detention Results for 25 Weeks: No Order Effect

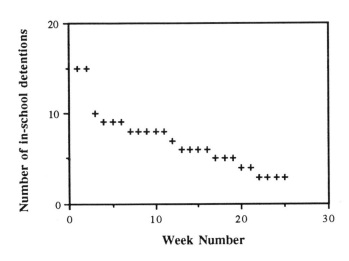

Figure 5.17. Sequence Plot of Detention Results for 25 Weeks: Decreasing Trend

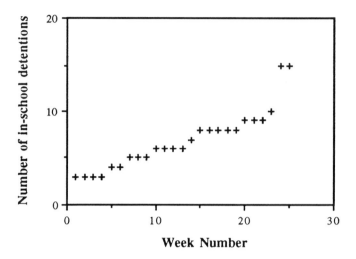

Figure 5.18. Sequence Plot of Detention Results for 25 Weeks: Increasing Trend

how the process actually works. Resolving the disagreements allows the team studying the process to agree about exactly what happens at each step of the process. Developing this consensus is essential before seeking to improve the process. After all, who knows a job better than those who do it?

Figure 5.19 presents an example of a flowchart describing the process used to classify work orders in a school maintenance department. The quality improvement team studying delays in the classification process was surprised to see how many steps there were in the process.

After doing this, the second step toward improving a process is to survey customers of that process to see what parts of the process are and are not working. Relative to the in-school detention system, one set of customers would be the teachers in the school. One could survey them and ask which parts of the in-school detention system are working and which ones aren't. The results of this survey could then be displayed in a bar chart in which the bars are ordered from the most frequently occurring problem to the least frequently

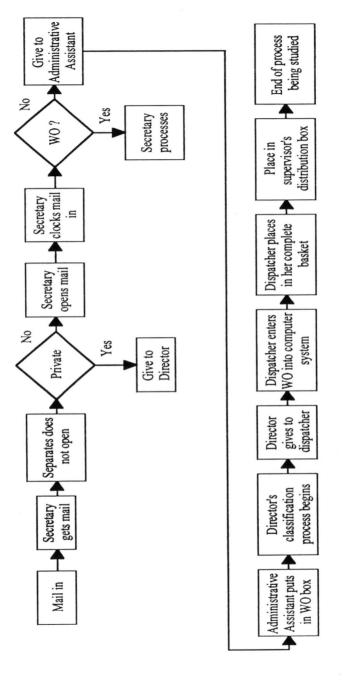

Figure 5.19. Process Flowchart for Mail-In Work Order

145

occurring one. This ordered bar chart is typically called a *Pareto diagram* (or *Pareto chart*). It identifies the most serious problems to be addressed and separates them from the others.

A perennial problem for maintenance workers is that of being asked by school personnel to do extra jobs, "now that you are at our school," above and beyond the jobs on the work order that the maintenance worker was sent to do. A quality improvement team studying this situation sent a questionnaire to a sample of workers asking what extra jobs they were asked to do. The results are summarized in the Pareto diagram in Figure 5.20. Moving furniture and unnecessary cleaning were the most frequent requests.

For the previous detention example, now suppose that a Pareto analysis indicates that the most problematic aspect of the in-school detention system is that the teachers are not receiving the paperwork back from the administration relative to what has happened to their students sent to in-school detention. The next step is to search for potential causes of this problem. A useful analysis tool here is the *cause-and-effect diagram* in which the members of the team investigating this problem brainstorm on what may have produced the absence of the paperwork. Generally, the categories in cause-and-effect diagrams are methods, materials, machines, personnel, environment, and measurement. After the cause-and-effect diagram is done, we may have identified some candidate solutions for improving the process.

Figure 5.21 illustrates an actual cause-and-effect diagram created by a team studying missing information on maintenance department work orders. The diagram reflects the team's assessment that the difficulty might be due to the personnel at the school not knowing what information the maintenance department required. Another potential (and related) source of the difficulty was thought to be lack of uniform format and instructions for communicating work orders to maintenance.

Before implementing a change in the process, it is useful to gather baseline data on the unchanged process so that we have an accurate moving picture of what is going on in the process now. Suppose that a baseline study produced the data in Table 5.4. Plotting that data in a sequence plot yields Figure 5.15. The questions that now arise are these: Is this process stable? Is it "in control"?

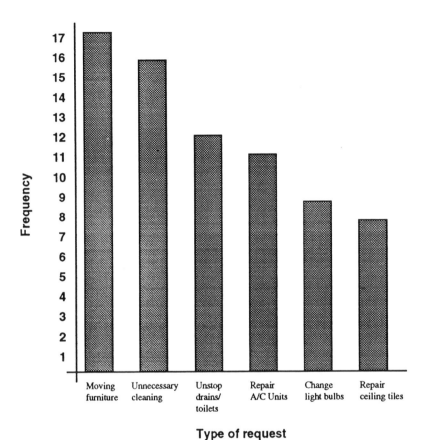

Figure 5.20. Pareto Chart of Responses to Questionnaire About Extra Work Requests

These are questions that one addresses by constructing a *control chart* for the percentage of students in the school who are placed on in-school detention in any one week. Procedures for doing this are described in Gitlow, Gitlow, Oppenheim, and Oppenheim (1989) and Nelson (1984).

We use control charts to see whether or not the points on the chart, the observations on the process, stay between the upper

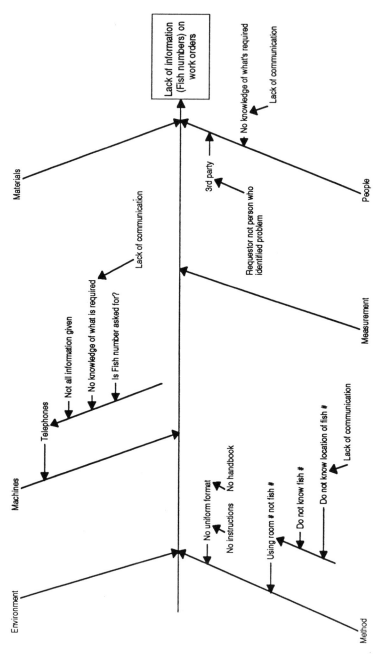

Figure 5.21. Cause-and-Effect Diagram Showing Potential Causes for Lack of Information on Work Orders

control limits (UCL) and lower control limits (LCL) (these are represented in Figure 5.22) or whether they exhibit some other nonrandom pattern. If the points stay within the control limits and do not exhibit any nonrandom patterns, the process is said to be "in control." There still is variation in the process, but it is variation that is a part of the process, a part of the in-school detention system in that school, and not variation resulting from shocks to the system. If the system is in control, then we can predict what we will expect to observe next week (provided that the system stays in control), namely, a result between the control limits.

In Figure 5.22, there are two points outside the control limits. When we investigate further, we discover that the first of these points was the first week of school in the fall, while the second of these points was the first week of school after Christmas vacation. The points outside the control limits indicate variation beyond that usually seen in the process. This extraneous variation is called "special cause variation."

In this case, the special cause of the two points outside the control limits appears to be that these two periods both are the first week that students are in school after being out of school for an extended period of time. Further study of these times shows that the paperwork associated with this process is seriously delayed at these times. Other than in these 2 weeks, the process appears to be in control.

Thus the decision may be made to implement a change in the in-school detention program so that the teachers quickly receive the paperwork on their students sent to detention. Suppose now that we observe the school for the remaining 10 weeks of the school year. The observations slowly drift down to a lower level than where they were before and stay at that lower level, as is reflected in Figure 5.23. This indicates that there has been a shift from the performance of the process from the first 25 weeks of the year. More timely paperwork appears to have had an impact on the process. Starting the next school year with the new paperwork management system shows promise of producing improvement in the in-school detention system.

This study of the in-school detention system has some weaknesses. For example, the difference observed may have been caused by some other factor, such as the fact that the end of the school year

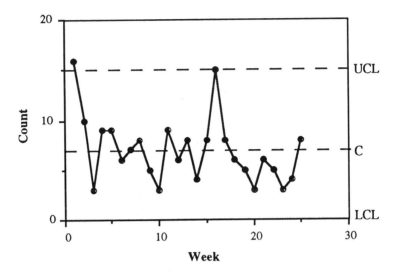

Figure 5.22. Control Chart of the Detention Results

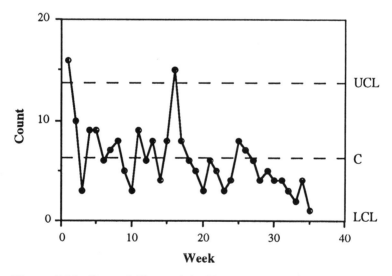

Figure 5.23. Control Chart of the Detention Results Including the Postintervention Counts

was approaching. Gaudard, Coates, and Freeman (1991) describe a more rigorous seven-step procedure for identifying the root cause of a quality problem:

1. Define the project.
2. Study the current situation.
3. Analyze the potential causes.
4. Implement a solution.
5. Check the results.
6. Standardize the improvement.
7. Establish future plans.

Another procedure for identifying and addressing gaps in a system's results, based on Kaufman (1992a), requires the following steps:

1. Identify the problem (based on needs).
2. Identify detailed requirements and possible solutions.
3. Select solutions (from alternatives).
4. Implement the solutions.
5. Determine effectiveness and efficiency.
6. Revise (continuously) as required.

These are rigorous tactics for finding the root cause of a quality problem. The study that we have just described that involved the paperwork change in the in-school detention program does not meet this standard. The question for the school administrator is whether this study as it stands provides enough evidence to indicate that it would be useful to adopt the new paperwork system for the next year. A potential plan of action is to adopt the system and continue to monitor the control chart for the number of in-school detentions per week.

An example. A school maintenance department launched a quality improvement initiative by doing a survey of the individuals it served to assess their satisfaction with various aspects of the services

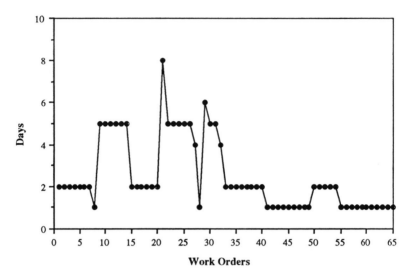

Figure 5.24. Sequence Plot of Days Required to Classify a Work Order

delivered. The results indicated that there was room for improvement in response time to routine maintenance calls. Of all the respondents, 22% felt neutral, somewhat dissatisfied, or very dissatisfied with these times.

The team then did a process flowchart of this process from the time the request reached the maintenance department until it was classified and assigned to a supervisor. The team constructed a cause-and-effect diagram to explore potential reasons for delays in classification time. They then decided to gather data for 3 weeks on days required for classification under the current system in which the head of the department does the classification. Then the manager of operations did the classifications for 4 weeks. The data are summarized in the sequence plot in Figure 5.24.

The head of the department classified the first 32 work orders and the manager of operations classified the remainder. This graph led to the responsibility for classification being shifted to the operations manager.

A Summary of Each Graph Used
and the Information It Generates

A *sequence plot* shows how an interval/ratio variable is changing over time.

A *histogram* shows the distribution of values of an interval/ratio variable.

A *bar chart* shows the distribution of values of a nominal/ordinal variable.

A *pie chart* shows the distribution of values of a nominal/ordinal variable.

A *side-by-side histogram* provides a comparison of the distributions of values of an interval/ratio variable for each of several values of a nominal/ordinal variable.

A *stacked bar histogram* provides a comparison of the distributions of values of an interval/ratio variable for each of several values of a nominal/ordinal variable.

A *scattergram* is a graph of the association between two interval/ratio variables.

A *Pareto diagram* is an indication of which of several problems is most severe and of the relative severity of all the problems.

A *cause-and-effect diagram* is a graphic of many potential causes of a problem organized by broad category: materials, methods, machines, measurements, personnel, and environment.

A *process flowchart* provides a picture of the sequence of steps involved in the process under study.

A *control chart* provides information on whether a process appears to be in control or out of control.

A Guide to Data-Based Decision Making

Here are some steps that will assist you in using data for decision making. Recall that "data-based decisions" is one of the clusters that Joiner has suggested.

1. Ask specific questions relative to mega-, macro-, and micro-level results, payoffs, and consequences. The seven basic questions are shown in Table 2.3. More detailed questions that reveal what to measure could be posed relative to each, such as the following:

   (a) How many of our completers are getting (macro level) and keeping jobs of their first, second, or third occupational choice (mega level)?

   (b) How many of our students have left before graduation, completion, or certification (macro)? How do these two groups differ on the basis of indicators of self-sufficiency and self-reliance (mega)?

   (c) How many of our graduates have entered a higher education program? How many are in undergraduate programs? How many are in vocational and technical programs? Are there any differences within and among these on the basis of variables including color, race, creed, sex, national origin (macro)?

   (d) How well are learners doing on accepted assessments of in-school performance, such as standardized tests (e.g., the SAT) (micro)?

   (e) How are learners progressing through the educational system, including promotion rates from grade level to grade level (micro)?

   (f) What are the truancy and tardiness rates of learners by grade levels (micro)?

2. For each question, identify valid, reliable, and unbiased methods and vehicles for collecting data. Any assessment vehicle (such as a test, questionnaire, or interview) might encompass one or more of the questions posed.

3. For each question and data collection vehicle, check to assure that answering each question will link to higher-order elements in the results chain (performance and the micro level

will contribute to macro-level results, and these in turn will contribute to mega-level consequences; for example, lowered detentions lead to better class and course content mastery, which leads to greater graduation/completion, which in turn leads to survival and self-sufficiency).

4. The answers for each question will provide useful data for decisions that will contribute to continuous improvement as you move relentlessly closer to reducing and closing gaps at the micro, macro, and mega levels of results.

5. Check to assure that the questions and assessment vehicles will provide unbiased, reliable, and valid criteria for evaluation.

6. Assure that evaluation data will be used only for continuous improvement, never for "making-wrong" or blaming.

Putting the Data to Work

It doesn't make much sense to sample, collect data, display them, and review them if we don't put the information to work to improve. While the entire system should strive for perfection, things do go wrong. We sometimes don't reach our objectives: to reduce or eliminate the needs.

We can use the information for "service recovery" (Berry & Parasuraman, 1991; Zemke & Bell, 1990): to make things right. When we view learners as one of our clients (not just something we do things to), we have to "do it right the second time around." When things go wrong, (a) admit it and apologize; (b) offer a solution for the shortfall, one that will work this time; (c) show *you* care, and show it by delivering on the solution; and (d) make an adjustment, if possible (perhaps by waiving a time limit violation you caused).

Data-based decisions can tell you what to fix (and why) and what to continue (and why). The general steps include collecting data on clients, identifying delivery/service problems, resolving problems effectively, learning from "recovery experiences," and modifying services/delivery (Berry & Parasuraman, 1991).

Note

1. Modern computer-driven statistical computing packages such as MINITAB, which is described by Schaefer and Farber (1992), also present additional numerical descriptive statistics that are less influenced by outlying observations than are the traditional mean or standard deviation. One of these is the *trimmed mean*, where the largest and smallest 5% of the observations are trimmed from the data set, so that the trimmed mean is based only on the central 90% of the data set. This produces a measure of location that is far less sensitive to a few "wild" observations than is the mean.

Dealing With Breakdowns
The Rest of the Story

Quality Improvement Efforts
Are Primarily Interpersonal
and Not Statistical

In the Public Broadcasting System series *Quality or Else* (Spring, 1992), David Langford, a leader of quality improvement efforts at Mount Edgecumbe High School in Sitka, Alaska, noted that when he began quality improvement activities he thought that 99% of the work would be statistical and 1% interpersonal. Now, after several years of working on quality improvement, he reports that his current opinion is that 1% of quality improvement work is statistical and 99% is interpersonal. Our experience matches his.

Breakdowns: A Challenge to Commitment to
One Team, Quality, and Data-Based Decisions

One of the toughest aspects of the interpersonal part of quality improvement is dealing with breakdown: any failure of a system to progress or function as intended. At least two broad classes of breakdowns occur. The first is the set of needs that are identified in the needs assessment part of quality improvement activities. Because a need is a gap between the desired and required results of a system, it is, by definition, a breakdown in the system.

The second class of breakdowns occurs when someone's expectations in an interaction are not matched by what actually happened in the interaction—when we use data to improve and when we have to work together.

The commitments to all on one team, quality, and data-based decisions are tested when data are collected that show needs—breakdowns in the current system—or when breakdowns occur in the internal operation of the team. Breakdowns also can occur when there are interactions among individuals in the organization—when not everyone is "singing from the same sheet of music."

We all are individuals with unique values, preferences, and experiences. When we are to work together, it is possible that these differences get in the way of our continuously moving toward a common destination.

Even when we have clear data on system performance (see Chapter 5), how we choose to interpret it and use it may make the difference between a quality effort that is shallow and one that makes a continuous contribution. If the quality team members treat all breakdowns—in the system and among people—in the same objective and caring manner, the resulting quality improvement will be impressive.

How well breakdowns of any sort are dealt with by a quality improvement team is an operational definition of "all on one team." Working together—not being resistive, territorial, or threatened—is so important that it is *Critical Success Factor 6*:

Building a cooperative team—whose members learn from each other and put the purposes of the QM+ effort above comfort and who continuously improve—is the key for moving from quality intention to realization.

Breakdowns and the Reactions to Them Are Predictable

Breakdowns can and do occur frequently in the operation of every quality improvement team. They show up in the team's interactions with its own members, with suppliers of information to the team, with the customers the team is seeking to serve, and with other individuals in the system, such as support staff or management. They may be small, as when one is 5 minutes late for an appointment, or large, as when a project is completed 6 months late and substantially over budget. Thus dealing with breakdowns and their consequences is a common task in any quality improvement team's life.

The typical responses to breakdowns are often one or more of the following:

- embarrassment
- guilt
- anger
- blame
- indignation
- confusion

- denial
- ridicule
- justification
- revenge
- excuses

Because quality improvement teams must deal with breakdowns in their own services (to which they might react strongly), and breakdowns in the services in the organization (to which others in the organization might react strongly), confronting them demands people skills in addition to technical skills. The teams also must have a clear understanding of the nature of breakdowns and their reactions to them as well as the specialized knowledge and skill necessary to interact sensibly and sensitively with others when breakdowns occur.

An essential piece of knowledge for dealing effectively with breakdowns is an awareness that the negative and ineffective defensive responses can be replaced by positive, effective responses:

- eager curiosity
- make it right
- let's learn from this one
- catch it now rather than being caught by it later
- problems don't cease to exist simply because you ignore them
- nobody's to blame, nobody's wrong
- joy
- growth
- learning
- satisfaction
- acceptance
- opportunity
- pride
- teamwork

This shift in responses dramatically improves the chances that the opportunity that is inherent in any breakdown can be discovered and acted upon effectively and efficiently.

Not Practicing What We Preach

Curiously, quality improvement teams usually do not systematically apply their own tools to the process of managing breakdowns. They do not gather reliable data about dealing with interpersonal breakdowns, nor do they analyze it and put the results to work—to improve.

This is particularly curious, given quality improvement team members' answers to the question, "What is the toughest problem you encounter in your team's work?" More than 90% of the time, responses have described interpersonal problems such as the following:

> The quality improvement team is not welcome by a shop supervisor because he or she is concerned that the team will be taking valuable time away from the work time of the individuals involved.

A principal agrees to a quality improvement initiative, has no questions about it, leaves the meeting in which this initiative is described, and then does not implement it or allow it to move forward.

The quality improvement team's efforts are thwarted by a lack of support from the school district's central administration.

The school board commits to quality improvement and then delegates it to the superintendent.

As the above situations indicate, there are interpersonal—human—problems associated with the success of quality improvement teams. Some interactions within the team as well as between the team and persons outside the team do not end to the satisfaction of all parties involved. Nor do these lead to quality. When this happens, a breakdown has occurred: a failure of a system to work or function properly.

Possibly, quality improvement teams have assumed (incorrectly) that the technical tools used for improving quality and productivity in technical operations are not useful for the interpersonal problems. Another possibility is that team members may unconsciously avoid using tools that might reveal a problem with their services. They are aware of the upset that often occurs when they discover a gap between desired and actual results of the system and they wish to avoid it.

Discussions with quality improvement teams about breakdowns and interpersonal problems indicate that, for one reason or another, many individuals appear to adopt the policy, "I'm not going to deal with these problems." Perhaps they are not dealing with such issues because they think, "It's not my job to deal with administrators who do not take my advice. It shouldn't be this way. I'll just do the technical aspects of my job as best I can and hope that these interpersonal problems will resolve themselves." Another possibility is that some may think, "I don't know what to do about interpersonal problems so I won't address them. Anyway, I have plenty of technical tasks that I do know how to do." Or some may just be too uncomfortable and run away.

Dealing Effectively With Breakdowns:
Six Steps

The following is our approach to improving how well one deals with breakdowns.[1] The heart of this approach is frankly realizing that, after becoming aware that a breakdown has occurred, we are each in an "emotional cloud" (which we all seem to enter upon discovering breakdowns in our lives) and are moving quickly and directly to lessen the intensity and duration of our emotional reactions. Realizing and admitting a problem are essential to solving it. The first five steps relate to attitudes and awareness; the sixth relates to data.

Attitudes and Awareness

(1) Accept that interpersonal problems are and will be present. Though this step may sound trivial, we present it to underscore how frequently we encounter the irrational point of view that interpersonal problems simply should not be present. It is critical to accept their presence as a first step toward dealing with them.

An example of this occurred recently in a conversation with an individual discussing difficult clients that he encountered on a daily basis. He reported he realized that his job was to deal with difficult clients. Anyone could deal with clients who had no problems and only want to order another copy of the company's software. Dealing with difficult clients with challenging questions was precisely the job he was hired for and his contribution to the company. He reported that when he realized that dealing with difficult clients was in fact his job—not just an ancillary annoyance—his perspective on these clients changed and he dealt with them more effectively.

(2) Adopt the point of view that interpersonal problems are problems whose solutions have not yet been discovered rather than being problems with no solutions. This involves setting aside certain points of view on interpersonal problems that are often present:

I do not have the time, energy, or other resources to deal with crisis situations (scarcity).

It is a tradition in our school district that the maintenance department and central administration do not work well together
(tradition).

There is no way to work with the principals in our district (no
solution).

Any one of these attitudes (scarcity, tradition, and no solution)
is a barrier to progress. There certainly is a deceptive safety in these
attitudes as well as risk in letting them go. Unfortunately, individuals
often do not see the benefit of shifting these points of view—adopting
a paradigm shift—until they become aware of the high price associated with maintaining them. For example, maintaining the attitude
that principals are uncooperative may well lead to one unsuccessful
meeting after another.

*(3) Adopt the point of view that an essential job for individuals on a
quality improvement team is* team building *and dealing with the associated relationship—all on one team—issues.* These issues involve individuals on and off the team. A successful relationship must be
established before technical information can be effectively gathered,
technical tools applied, and results implemented. Unless the interpersonal issues are effectively resolved, the quality of subsequent
quality improvement efforts is likely to be severely compromised.

*(4) Become aware that breakdowns occur in many aspects of life and
that initial reactions to these breakdowns tend to be negative, defensive, and
ineffective.* Breakdowns can and do occur at one time or another in
virtually all aspects of a quality improvement operation. Thus dealing with breakdowns and their complications is a frequent task in
any quality improvement team's life. What's real is real. Denying a
problem doesn't make it go away.

Our first response to any breakdown is to see it as a negative
experience to be avoided at any cost. Given the intensity of these
responses, there is no guarantee that the opportunity hidden in any
quality problem (a breakdown) will be realized. Part of the difficulty
is that a quality problem is only seen as a breakdown and people
initially react in ineffective ways to breakdowns.

(5) Shift one's attitude toward breakdowns from embarrassment, guilt, anger, and defensiveness to one of curiosity. Cultivating an attitude of eager curiosity rather than annoyance can then lead to exploring what the sources of the breakdown are so you can find ways to address them. Note that we are suggesting more than a shift from a negative attitude toward breakdowns to a positive attitude. In addition, we suggest becoming curious about breakdowns and pursuing questions such as the following:

> What was your experience of the meeting in which the breakdown occurred? What is your best guess of the other individual's experience of it? What was he or she feeling?
>
> What was your purpose in this meeting? The other individual's?
>
> What precisely do you see as the breakdown? (This question is particularly critical.)
>
> What can be learned from this breakdown?
>
> How do you suppose it happened?
>
> Is there any part of this meeting that you would now do differently?

Note that this step is an intrapersonal one and involves a shift in one's own attitude toward breakdowns. This is an essential step for individuals on the team to take before the team as a whole can effectively interact with breakdowns.

(6) Apply quality improvement tools to the team's activities and services, especially when breakdowns occur. In other words, gather data on how members of the team deal with breakdowns. Study either the needs that they encounter and reactions to those needs or the breakdowns in interactions either on the team or with individuals outside the team.[2] Gathering high quality data on the breakdown is an essential step toward improving how well the team deals with breakdowns—team building through stark, objective reality, which is addressed compassionately.

Remember that the heart of quality improvement activities is a commitment to continuous improvement. This includes a commitment to improving the process for dealing with breakdowns.

The process just described embodies one more of the paradigm shifts involved in moving from classical education to QM+. Several of these shifts are summarized in Figure 6.1.

Applying Quality Improvement Tools to Breakdowns

Implementing Step 6 is a major task facing every quality improvement team. The team must effectively deal with breakdowns as soon as they become apparent. If the team is to be effective in improving quality (based on its commitments to one team, passion for quality, and data-based decisions), team members must apply continuous improvement thinking and action to the team itself.

Applying quality improvement tools to a quality improvement team and its process for dealing with different types of breakdowns is a challenge. Again, we find that there is a sequence of steps to accomplish this.

(1) Become a participant in the process of improving the quality of the team's resolution of breakdowns rather than being a spectator who groans about the results not being satisfactory. Then, reflect and write completely what commitments to quality you have that are leading you to be a participant on this quality improvement team. What is it that you hope to build if this team is successful in this project? What considerations do you have about issues that may arise on the journey with the team? What do you stand for and how will you be able to produce the results that you stand for more effectively and more efficiently when this quality improvement team completes the project that it is currently engaged in?

(2) Develop a quality system to gather data (perhaps using video-tape) on how well your team deals with breakdowns. This system may involve videotaping team meetings in which needs that have been identified are examined to develop an action plan for reducing the needs. Videotape may also be useful for data describing breakdowns that occur during the team meeting itself as members are frustrated with some members of the team who consistently come late to the meetings or miss the meetings or who do not get

	Classical Education	QM+ Education
Relations Between Educator and Learner	• *Talk to* • *Knowledge dispenser* • *Monitor* • *Critic* • *Control*	• *Talk with* • *Information sharing* • *Coach* • *Helper* • *Empower*
Delivery	• *Courses teacher centered* • *Tests* • *Try harder*	• *Learning paths learner centered* • *Feedback for continuous growth* • *Work "smarter"*
Purpose	• *Pass courses, graduate* • *Short term* • *Competition* • *School*	• *Competence, confidence, and caring after learning* • *Long range* • *Cooperation* • *Society*
Planning	• *Units, courses, levels* • *Process/compliance* • *Courses, tests, subjects*	• *Continuity toward societal contribution* • *Results/contribution* • *Alignment, synergy, growth*
Evaluation	• *Scores, blame* • *Pass/fail* • *Compliance*	• *Guidance, help* • *Learn, improve* • *Achieve*
Motivation	• *External*	• *Internal*
Breakdown	• *Avoid*	• *Curiously seek out*

Figure 6.1. Comparing Classical Education With "QM+"

an assignment done on time. All breakdowns must be addressed effectively if the team is to make its contribution to the improvement of quality in the organization.

(3) Have each member of the team write his or her individual criteria for success in the breakdown process. Possibly the criteria might be different when dealing with breakdowns in the form of needs that have been identified as opposed to dealing with breakdowns in the quality team's processes.

(4) After a team meeting that involved dealing with breakdowns, invite the team members privately or in small groups to review the session before gathering the entire team to look at the quality of the breakdown management process. Ask each individual to identify places where the session was not progressing as well as at least that person intended for it to be progressing. Also ask each person to identify places where the process was working effectively and efficiently.

(5) Gather the team together after each person has identified where the meeting was and was not working. Do a Pareto analysis of the points where the meeting was not working in the eyes of the participants and a Pareto analysis of the parts of the meeting where the process was working. For example, the first Pareto analysis would involve listing all parts of the meeting where at least one team member did not think the meeting was working. Then the members would be polled to find out how many thought the individual parts were not working. Then we will know where the most frequently perceived breakdowns are.

Identify what is now being well done by the team and take steps to institutionalize that as a part of future meetings. Scrutinize places where the process has broken down. Discuss how you think a breakdown has occurred, being careful to avoid finding fault or blaming other individuals (such as top management or workers who may not be represented on the team).

(6) Keep looking for missing or ineffective skills, knowledge, attitudes, or abilities among the team members that may have contributed to the breakdown. When skills are lacking, acquire them through training, reading, workshops, consultants. Identify tactics for obtaining these missing or ineffective skills, knowledge, attitudes, or abilities. Develop exercises where the team members have the opportunity to practice using the new skills, knowledge, attitudes, or abilities that they are developing as a part of this process.

(7) Continue the process of improving how well your team deals with breakdowns that occur in its work by agreeing on when the next meeting is to be reviewed (and perhaps videotaped) and analyzed. A QM+ team is a learning team.

Costs Versus Benefits

Yes, this process for improving the quality of the team's dealing with breakdowns is time consuming. The consequences of not dealing with breakdowns effectively, however, are even more time consuming; breakdowns that are not dealt with will eat away at the team's commitment to quality, its commitment to being all on one team, and its commitment to data-based decisions.

This is another one of those places where a choice cannot be avoided. Either the team will choose to devote the time and energy to improving the quality of its breakdown resolution process or it will choose not to do this, either by action or by inaction. In either case, breakdowns will continue to occur. The only question is how well the team will deal with them. Figure 6.2 presents a process flow diagram for the activities of a functional team.

Notes

1. Several aspects of our approach are based on concepts in Communication Courses I and II taught by Landmark Education Corporation of San Francisco.

2. Often, the most powerful data are gathered by using videotape. This may involve videotaping team meetings in which needs that have been identified are examined so as to develop an action plan for reducing the needs. Videotape also may be useful for data describing breakdowns that occur during the team meeting itself as members are frustrated with some members of the team who consistently come late to the meetings or miss the meetings or who do not get an assignment done on time. Individuals are often uncomfortable with this process until they have made the shift in attitude toward breakdown described in Step 5. Zahn (1988) describes the use of videotape to improve the quality of one's process for dealing with breakdowns.

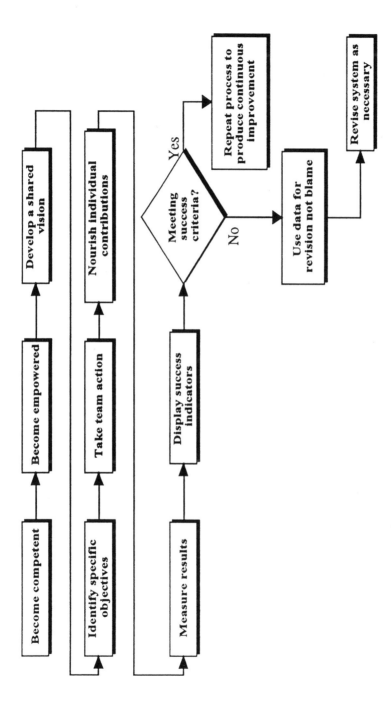

Figure 6.2. Process Flow Diagram for Activities of a Functional Team

169

Put It All to Work

The Basic Tools and Concepts of
Quality Management Plus

Quality education is possible. Learner success, in school and in life, is possible. Our shared social and economic future depends on turning the possibility into reality by continuously improving our results and contributions. Delivering to education's clients what they can really use, when they can use it, and in a form that is usable is within our reach. It only takes the vision, will, and skill to define and continuously achieve quality.

We have supplied the what's, why's, and how's of QM and QM+. QM+ is a practical and rational process for delivering the kind of education required for tomorrow's children. Six critical success factors can guide you through every step and phase of defining and creating quality in education:

1. Be willing to move out of today's comfort zones and use new and wider boundaries for thinking, planning, doing, and evaluating.

2. Use and link all three levels of results (mega, macro, and micro) for defining and delivering quality.

3. Everyone demonstrates a passion for quality; everything everyone does, constantly and consistently, is directed toward improving the quality of what is used, done, and delivered.

4. Everyone—learners, teachers, administrators, parents, employers, neighbors—is on the same team. Quality is what everyone is after, and everyone will make a unique and collective contribution to achieve it.

5. All decisions are made on the basis of solid, objective, relevant performance data.

6. Building a cooperative team—whose members learn from each other and put the purposes of the QM+ effort above comfort and who continuously improve—is the key to moving from quality intention to realization.

The Basis for a QM Audit

Each time you and the quality team meet, make a decision, and take any action, check each of the six critical success factors. You could use the critical success factors as the basis for a quick audit of your QM program.

Applying the Basics of This Book

In each chapter, we provided concepts, tools, and guidance that will allow the six success factors to be applied.

- *Chapter 1*: The basic elements of quality management (QM); Deming's 14 points and how to put them to work; what a quality team does and delivers; what is quality; quality management as a commitment to a better future and a transformation, not just another program

- *Chapter 2*: The building blocks of QM, that is, what's involved; changing the way we view the world and shifting our paradigms and our mental gears, including how we view and interact with our world; the three levels of educational results of mega, macro, and micro; the Organizational Elements Model (OEM); ends and means; defining need; doing a needs assessment for quality management initiatives; opportunities; strategic and tactical planning and their relationship to QM; putting Deming's principles to work in education

- *Chapter 3*: What is involved in implementing QM in your school or district and some additional specifics for implementing QM:

  - Steps 1 and 2: The decision and commitment to quality
  - Step 3: Selecting the quality level
  - Step 4: Defining the ideal
  - Step 5: Assessing needs
  - Steps 6 and 7: Allocating the meeting of needs and identifying and selecting ways of meeting needs
  - Step 8: Installing and institutionalizing
  - Step 9: Continuous progress and contribution; awards and certification; keeping QM elements in balance; how to keep QM from failing

- *Chapter 4*: Adding the mega level to QM to get quality management plus (QM+); what's to be gained by using QM+; QM, QM+, strategic planning, strategic planning plus (SP+), and continuous improvement; our ethical and practical choice; the boundaries of QM+

- *Chapter 5:* The importance of high quality data in decision making; the quality system as a vital part of QM and QM+; decisions, facts, and continuous improvement; basic statistical tools; the study of a population; the study of a process; a guide to data-based decision making; putting the data to work

- *Chapter 6:* Quality improvement efforts, human contributions, and statistics; breakdowns; commitment to quality, one team, and data-based decisions; practicing what we preach;

predictable reactions to breakdowns; dealing effectively with breakdowns; applying quality improvement tools to breakdowns; costs versus benefits

Delivering on the Promise of QM+

Above all, QM+ is a process for transforming educational inputs into useful results and payoffs. We realize the transformation through what we use, how we use it, and what we deliver. People, competent and caring individuals, make the difference between a quality process that delivers on its rich promise or deteriorates into another going-through-the-motions exercise. QM+ is a way of thinking, acting, interacting, delivering.

When forming a QM+ team, these considerations—in question form—will focus on defining quality:

1. Who are our clients?
2. What would client satisfaction look like, and how would we measure it?
3. What characteristics of the outputs (graduates, completers, and so on) of the educational system would deliver client satisfaction? How would we measure it?
4. What are the building-block results (mastery in courses, abilities, skills, knowledge, and so on) that we would deliver as identified in 3 and 2, above, and how would we measure each?
5. What are the activities (courses, programs, activities, and so on) that would deliver the building-block results identified in 4, and what are the specifications for each?
6. What resources, including people, facilities, funds, learner entry characteristics, are required to do what is identified in 5 to deliver the results in 4?
7. What must each person do, continuously, to make certain that 6, 5, 4, 3, and 2 happen effectively and efficiently?
8. What data are required for making decisions on how things are progressing: what to keep, what to change, what to stop?
9. Have we applied all six critical success factors?

There are nine commitment/action elements we suggest to guide your QM+ team as they implement the concepts and tools of this book to deliver quality and continuous improvement:

1. Make the decision.
2. Commit to quality.
3. Select the quality level.
4. Define the ideal.
5. Assess needs.
6. Allocate the meeting of needs.
7. Identify and select ways of meeting needs.
8. Install and institutionalize.
9. Continue to progress and contribute.

Specifically, the successful quality team will use the following steps to guide the continuous improvement of education:

(1) Define the ideal mega-level vision: the world in which we want tomorrow's child to live. Identify only results and conditions and do not include processes, resources, or methods. The extent to which the planning partners make this speak to results, not to favored initiatives or methods, is the degree to which this step will be useful.

(2) Determine gaps between current conditions and the ideal vision.

(3) Obtain agreement, based on the ideal vision, from the planning partners on what would deliver client satisfaction for future and closer-in years (year 2000, 1995, next year) and agree on how we would measure it. Identify the predicted needs—gaps in results—for each target year.

(4) Define and specify the characteristics of the outputs of the educational system that would lead to clients' satisfaction and how we would measure it.

(5) Define and specify the building-block results (mastery in courses, abilities, skills, knowledge, and so on) that we would deliver to achieve Steps 1 and 2, above. Define how we would measure each.

(6) Specify the activities (courses, initiatives, activities, and so on) that would deliver the building-block results and what the specifications are for each.

(7) Specify the resources—including people, facilities, funds, learner entry characteristics—required to deliver and complete the activities necessary to deliver the required results.

(8) Specify what each person must do, continuously, to make certain that quality results and activities happen effectively and efficiently. Extend the quality system to include mega-level criteria and results that will be used by the QM team members.

(9) Collect data on progress toward the ideal vision (defined in Step 1) and progress toward yearly objectives (in Step 3). Add mega-level variables and criteria to the possible variables already identified for QM. The exact criteria and variables to be part of the quality system should be determined by your QM team. When selecting variables, be sure to identify indicators that will be an accurate and complete representation of all that education uses, does, accomplishes, and delivers as well as the societal and community payoffs.

(10) Identify which educational activities and initiatives should be continued and which are to be revised to achieve useful quality.

(11) Revise as required, and continue what is working.

Quality management depends upon forming a partnership of diverse individuals who want to see good things happen for learners. Successful QM+ partnerships have the following characteristics; work and share with each other using these basic principles:

1. Everyone agrees to work together as they move toward a common destination.
2. Each individual is important and is expected to make a contribution toward the shared effort.
3. Each person provides support and assistance, when asked, to others.
4. Everyone is honest with themselves and each other.
5. Data collection, evaluation, and feedback are used for improving, never for blaming. Everyone learns from mistakes and experiences.
6. Objectives are stated clearly, concisely, and without confusion.

7. Means and resources are selected based upon the results to be obtained, not the other way around.

8. There is no limit to what can be accomplished if people don't have to own and get credit for their ideas.

9. Constant progress and cooperation characterize everyone's day-to-day efforts and contributions. Everyone looks for opportunities for successful action.

Using Quality Management Plus in Your School or System

Quality management processes may be applied throughout any educational system. Regardless of your starting point in the system—of course, we urge the mega level as the starting place—the basics of quality management are useful. Quality education depends upon a common, shared destination, a passion for quality, everyone working on one team toward the shared destination, and a quality system that allows all quality team members to constantly and continuously improve. If any one element is favored over the others, then quality will suffer.

The quality system—the basis for data-based decisioning—is missing in most educational systems. While educators collect some data (test scores, grade point averages, truancy rates, and so on), there is not a consistent tracking of important variables. Missing are the data that will allow the quality partners, including learners, to identify what is working and what is not as they move relentlessly toward the ideal vision.

Chapter 5 identified what data could be collected and how to make sense of it. Chapter 6 shared how to deal with breakdowns; what to do when we are below our quality standards. One more bridge between planning and quality is missing: how to meet needs through learning experiences.

Applying quality principles to educational design and development. Data are useless by themselves. We can and should use needs data—gaps between current results and desired ones—to design, develop, implement, and evaluate learning experiences and organizational contributions. The area of greatest attention in any educational system is the performance of learners. If quality is to become a reality, it will be seen in what learners know, in what they can accomplish, and in how well they apply their abilities in school and in later life. Instruction, successful instruction, is the heart of any educational system. Quality management can be applied to educational design and development, and the six critical success factors should be applied. Let's see how this works.

A natural fit exists between the concepts of quality management and educational system planning and instructional systems development (e.g., American National Standards Institute, 1992). System planning identifies where a system should be headed and identifies the requirements with which to measure success. Chapter 2 provided the basics on system thinking and the importance of relating three levels of educational system contributions: mega, macro, and micro. Instructional systems design and development (ISDD) (e.g., Branson et al., 1975; Dick & Carey, 1989) is a rigorous process by which performance specifications, usually at the micro level, are fashioned into learning systems that work. ISDD has been applied to an increasing number of education and training environments and demonstrates that we can measurably improve learner performance.[1]

Quality management in general, and the quality system (Chapter 5) in particular, can contribute the data bases for ISDD. By identifying the basic elements in designing and delivering effective learning experiences, the quality team can use such standards to track how well they are doing as they pursue continuous improvement. The American National Standards Institute Accredited Standards Committee Z-1 on quality assurance has developed preliminary standards for learner performance systems (American National Standards Institute, 1992). Based on industrial quality standards (ANSI/ASQC Q91), a working group has developed a guidance process for assuring that achieving quality for learners will result.[2]

The development of learning materials that will be effective and efficient starts with the identified needs (best derived from the gaps in results at the mega, macro, and then micro levels) and then progresses to the various steps for instructional systems design, development, delivery, evaluation, and revision. Figure 7.1 shows a flowchart suggested by the Z-1 study committee.

There is, and should be, a consistent, data-referenced flow from needs to performance specifications, to design specifications, to learning system design and development, to evaluation and revision. The process is similar to system engineering processes that have been so successful in business and industry. This process puts the learners' success in central focus and actually designs (and tailor makes) learning experiences that will be effective and efficient.

In using a systematic design of instruction approach, the three basic ingredients of quality management are present: a passion for quality (get important, shared results), all on one team (to deliver learner performance and system contributions), and data-based decision making (for defining learning requirements and using these to select, develop, and evaluate how learning takes place).

The Challenge

QM+ in education is both practical and ethical. This is an area where choice can't be avoided. If you say "no" to QM+, what else do you have in mind? What strategy will you implement to address concerns about education? Our futures depend on your choice.

We invite and encourage you and your colleagues to join together with all your education partners to implement QM+ in your schools. We close with questions from John F. Kennedy: If not you, who? If not now, when?

Notes

1. Instructional systems design and development (ISDD) has usually been applied only at the micro level. The concepts used in ISDD are, however, generalizable to organizational and even societal concerns. The basic elements include basic problem identification and resolution, including (a) identifying opportunities and problems (based on needs); (b) determining detailed requirements and identifying alternative ways and means to meet the requirements;

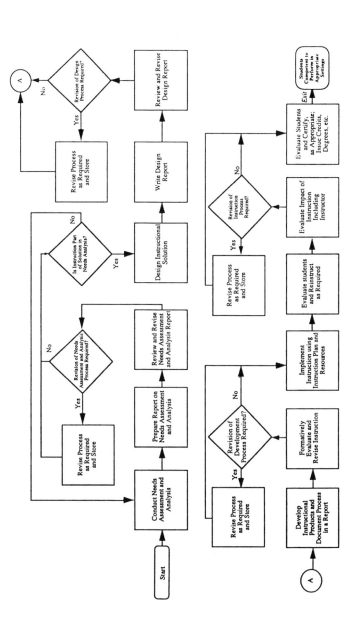

Figure 7.1. Flowchart of the Systematic Design of Instruction

SOURCE: From the American National Standards Institute Accredited Standards Committee Z-1 on quality assurance (draft, September 9, 1992); used by permission.

(c) selecting ways and means based on return on investment; (d) implementing; (e) determining performance effectiveness and efficiency; and (f) revising whenever and wherever required (Kaufman, 1992a). Whether we are improving the quality of instruction or the quality of the payoffs for tomorrow's children, QM+ and a generalized form of ISDD/problem solving are useful.

2. The dimensions reported include management responsibility; quality system; contract review; design control; document control; purchasing; purchaser supplied product; product identification and traceability; process control; inspection and testing; inspection, measuring, and test equipment; inspection and test status; control of nonconforming product; corrective action; handling, storage, packaging, and delivery; quality records; internal quality audits; training; servicing; statistical techniques. While these "smack" of classical quality control/quality assurance labels and concepts, they are intended to define the elements of a successful quality system implementation. Their applicability to education is clear.

References

Ackoff, R. L., & Sasieni, M. W. (1968). *Fundamentals of operations research.* New York: John Wiley.

American National Standards Institute. (1992, September 9). *Quality systems: Requirements for using quality principles in education and training* (American National Standard draft document: ANSI/ ASQC Z-1.11 1992). Milwaukee, WI: American Society for Quality Control, Accredited Standards Committee Z-1 on Quality Assurance.

Banathy, B. H. (1991). *Systems design of education: A journey to create the future.* Englewood Cliffs, NJ: Educational Technology.

Berry, L. L., & Parasuraman, A. (1991). *Marketing services.* New York: Free Press.

Bhote, K. R. (1989, Autumn). The Malcolm Baldrige Quality Award. *National Productivity Review, 8*(4).

Branson, R. K. (1988). Why schools can't improve: The upper limit hypothesis. *Journal of Instructional Development, 10*(4), 15-26.

Branson, R. K., et al. (1975, August). *Interservice procedures for instructional systems development* (Phases I, II, III, IV, V, and Executive Summary) (U.S. Army Training and Doctrine Command Pamphlet 350). Fort Monroe, VA: U.S. Army.

Buckley, W. (Ed.). (1968). *Modern systems research for the behavioral scientist.* Chicago: Aldine.

Carter, L. F. (1969). *The systems approach to education: The mystique and the reality* (Report SP-3921). Los Angeles: System Development Corporation.

Checkland, P. (1981). *Systems thinking, systems practice.* New York: John Wiley.

Cleland, D. I., & King, W. R. (1968). *Systems analysis and project management.* New York: McGraw-Hill.

Conner, D. R. (in press). *Managing at the speed of sound.* New York: Villard (division of Harper & Row).

Cook, W. J., Jr. (1990). *Bill Cook's strategic planning for America's schools* (rev. ed.). Birmingham, AL: Cambridge Management Group, Inc.; Arlington, VA: American Association of School Administrators.

Crosby, P. B. (1979). *Quality is free: The art of making quality certain.* New York: McGraw-Hill.

Cuban, L. (1990, January). Reforming again, again, and again. *Educational Researcher,* pp. 3-13.

Deming, W. E. (1986). *Out of the crisis.* Cambridge: MIT, Center for Advanced Engineering Technology.

Deming, W. E. (1990, May 10). *A system of profound knowledge* (Personal memo). Washington, DC.

Det norske Veritas Industry. (n.d.-a). *Accredited quality system certification.* Houston, TX: Author.

Det norske Veritas Industry. (n.d.-b). *9000 & 9: Most often asked questions on ISO 9000.* Houston, TX: Author.

DeYoung, H. G. (1990, February 19). Tiny resistor maker keeps its eyes on the Baldrige prize. *Electronic Business.*

Dick, W., & Carey, L. (1989). *The systematic design of instruction* (3rd ed.). Glenview, IL: Scott, Foresman.

Dillman, D. A. (1978). *Mail and telephone surveys: The total design method.* New York: John Wiley.

Drucker, P. (1992, September-October). The new society of organizations. *Harvard Business Review.*

Feigenbaum, A. V. (1951). *Quality control principles, practice, and administration.* New York: McGraw-Hill.

Galagan, P. A. (1991, June). How Wallace changed its mind. *Training & Development, 45*(6).

Gaudard, M., Coates, R., & Freeman, L. (1991, October). Accelerating improvement. *Quality Progress,* pp. 81-88.

Gilbert, T. F. (1978). *Human competence: Engineering worthy performance.* New York: McGraw-Hill.

Gilbert, T. F., & Gilbert, M. B. (1989, January). Performance engineering: Making human productivity a science. *Performance & Instruction.*

Gitlow, H., Gitlow, S., Oppenheim, A., & Oppenheim, R. (1989). *Tools and methods for the improvement of quality.* Homewood, IL: Irwin.

Hintzen, N. (1990, September). An approach to conducting follow-up on vocational students: Implications for educational planning. *Performance & Instruction.*

Imai, M. (1986). *Kaizen: The key to Japan's competitive success.* New York: McGraw-Hill.

Joiner, B. L. (1985, August). The key role of statisticians in the transformation of North American industry. *The American Statistician, 39*(3).

Joiner, B. L. (1986, May). Using statisticians to help transform industry in America. *Quality Progress,* pp. 46-50.

Juran, J. (1979). *Quality control handbook* (3rd ed.). New York: McGraw-Hill.

Kanter, R. M. (1989). *When giants learn to dance: Mastering the challenges of strategy, management, and careers in the 1990's.* New York: Simon & Schuster.

Kaufman, R. (1972). *Educational systems planning.* Englewood Cliffs, NJ: Prentice-Hall.

Kaufman, R. (1988a). *Planning educational systems: A results-based approach.* Lancaster, PA: Technomic.

Kaufman, R. (1988b, September). Preparing useful performance indicators. *Training & Development Journal.*

Kaufman, R. (1991, December). Toward total quality "plus." *Training.*

Kaufman, R. (1992a). *Strategic planning plus: An organizational guide* (rev. ed.). Newbury Park, CA: Sage.

Kaufman, R. (1992b). *Mapping educational success.* Newbury Park, CA: Corwin.

Kaufman, R. (1992c, April). The challenge of total quality management in education. *International Journal of Educational Reform.*

Kaufman, R. (1992d, May). Six steps to strategic success. *Training and Development.*

Kaufman, R. (1992e, July). The magnifying glass mentality. *Performance & Instruction Journal.*

Kaufman, R., & Herman, J. (1991). *Strategic planning in education: Rethinking, restructuring, revitalizing.* Lancaster, PA: Technomic.

Kaufman, R., Rojas, A. M., & Mayer, H. (1993). *Needs assessment: A user's guide.* Englewood Cliffs, NJ: Educational Technology.

Kaufman, R., & Valentine, G. (1989, November). Relating needs assessment and needs analysis. *Performance & Instruction Journal.*

Kirst, M. W., & Meister, G. R. (1985, Summer). Turbulence in American secondary schools: What reforms last? *Curriculum Inquiry, 15*(2).

Kuhn, T. (1962). *The structure of scientific revolution.* Chicago: University of Chicago Press.

Kuhn, T. (1970). *The structure of scientific revolution* (2nd ed.). Chicago: University of Chicago Press.

Lawton, R. L. (1991, September). Creating a customer-centered culture in service industries. *Quality Progress*, pp. 69-72.

MacGillis, P., Hintzen, N., & Kaufman, R. (1989). Problems and prospects of implementing a holistic planning framework in vocational education: Applications of the organizational elements model (OEM). *Performance Improvement Quarterly, 2*(1).

Mager, R. F. (1961). *Setting instructional objectives.* Palo Alto, CA: Fearon.

Mager, R. F. (1975). *Preparing instructional objectives* (2nd ed.). Belmont, CA: David S. Lake.

Marquardt, D., Chove, J., Jensen, K. E., Petrick, K., Pyle, J., & Strahle, D. (1991, May). Vision 2000: The strategy for the ISO 9000 Series standards in the '90s. *Quality Progress*, pp. 25-31.

Milliken & Company. (1990). *Quality leadership through research.* Spartanburg, SC: Author.

Moore, D. S. (1991). *Statistics: Concepts and controversies* (3rd ed.). New York: Freeman.

Morgan, R. M., & Chadwick, C. B. (1971). *Systems analysis for educational change: The Republic of Korea.* Tallahassee: Florida State University, Department of Educational Research.

Naisbitt, J., & Aburdene, P. (1990). *Megatrends 2000: Ten new directions for the 1990's.* New York: William Morrow.

Nelson, F. H. (1992, July). The myth of high public spending on American education. *International Journal of Educational Reform.*

Nelson, L. S. (1984, October). The Shewhart Control Chart: Tests for special causes. *Journal of Quality Technology, 16,* 237-239.

Newmann, F. M. (1991). Linking restructuring to authentic student achievement. *Phi Delta Kappan, 72*(6), 458-463.

Oberle, J. (1990, January). Quality gurus: The men and their messages. *Training.*

Osborne, D., & Gaebler, T. (1992). *Reinventing government: How the entrepreneurial spirit is transforming the public sector.* Reading, MA: Addison-Wesley.

Perelman, L. J. (1990, May). *The "acanemia" deception* (Briefing Paper No. 120). Indianapolis, IN: Hudson Institute.

Pfeiffer, J. W., Goodstein, L. D., & Nolan, T. M. (1989). *Shaping strategic planning: Frogs, bees, and turkey tails.* Glenview, IL: Scott, Foresman.

Pipho, C. (1991, February). Business leaders focus on reform. *Phi Delta Kappan,* pp. 422-423.

Rasell, E., & Mishel, L. (1990, January). *Shortchanging education.* Washington, DC: Economic Policy Institute.

Rummler, G. A., & Brache, A. P. (1990). *Improving performance: How to manage the white space on the organization chart.* San Francisco: Jossey-Bass.

Schaefer, R. L., & Farber, E. (1992). *The student edition of MINITAB user's manual.* Reading, MA: Addison-Wesley.

Schaeffer, R., Mendenhall, W., & Ott, L. (1990). *Elementary survey sampling* (4th ed.). Boston: PWS-Kent.

Senge, P. M. (1990). *The fifth discipline: The art & practice of the learning organization.* New York: Doubleday-Currency.

Shewhart, W. A. (1931). *Economic control of quality of manufactured product.* New York: Van Nostrand.

Sobel, I., & Kaufman, R. (1989). Toward a "hard" metric for educational utility. *Performance Improvement Quarterly, 2*(1).

Taguchi, G., & Phadke, M. S. (1984). Quality engineering through design optimization. In *Proceedings of Globecome 84 Meeting.* New York: IEEE Communication Society.

Toffler, A. (1990). *Powershift: Knowledge, wealth, and violence at the edge of the 21st century.* New York: Bantam.

U.S. General Accounting Office. (1991, May). *Management practices: U.S. companies improve performance through quality efforts* (GAO/NSIAD-91-190). Washington, DC: Author.

Von Bertalanffy, L. (1968). General system theory: A critical review. In W. Buckley (Ed.), *Modern systems theory for the behavioral scientist.* Chicago: Aldine.

Weiers, R. M. (1991). *Introduction to business statistics.* Chicago: Dryden.

Zahn, D. A. (1988). Quality breakdowns: An opportunity in disguise. In *Forty-Second Annual Quality Congress Transactions* (pp. 56-62). Milwaukee, WI: American Society for Quality Control.

Zemke, R., & Bell, C. (1990, June). Service recovery: Doing it right the second time. *Training.*

Suggested Readings

American Society for Quality Control. (1987, June 19). *Quality systems: Model for quality assurance in design/development, production, installation, and servicing* (American National Standard: ANSI/ASQC Q91-1987). Milwaukee, WI: Author.

Banathy, B. (1987). Instructional systems design. In R. M. Gagne (Ed.), *Instructional technology: Foundations*. Hillsdale, NJ: Lawrence Erlbaum.

Bhote, K. R. (1989, Autumn). The Malcolm Baldrige Quality Award. *National Productivity Review, 8*(4).

Briggs, L. J., & Wager, W. W. (1982). *Handbook of procedures for the design of instruction* (2nd ed.). Englewood Cliffs, NJ: Educational Technology.

Caplan, F. (1990). *The quality system: A sourcebook for managers and engineers*. Radnor, PA: Chilton.

Conner, D. (1992, April 1). *Senior management's role when implementing change*. One-day executive briefing for Florida's SchoolYear 2000

Project, Florida State University, Tallahassee, Learning Systems Institute, Center for Educational Technology.

Corrigan, R. E., & Corrigan, B. O. (1985). *SAFE: System approach for effectiveness.* New Orleans, LA: R. E. Corrigan Associates.

Deming, W. E. (1982). *Quality, productivity, and competitive position.* Cambridge: MIT, Center for Advanced Engineering Study.

Gagne, R. M., & Briggs, L. J. (1979). *Principles of instructional design* (2nd ed.). New York: Holt, Rinehart & Winston.

Gagne, R. M., Briggs, L. J., & Wager, W. W. (1988). *Principles of instructional design* (3rd ed.). New York: Holt, Rinehart & Winston.

Galagan, P. A. (1991, October). The learning organization made plain (Interview with P. Senge). *Training & Development, 45*(10).

Gilbert, T. F. (1971). Mathetics: The technology of education. In M. D. Merrill (Ed.), *Instructional design: Readings.* Englewood Cliffs, NJ: Prentice-Hall.

Harless, J. H. (1975). *An ounce of analysis is worth a pound of cure.* Newnan, GA: Harless Performance Guild.

Harless, J. H. (1986). Guiding performance with job aids. In M. Smith (Ed.), *Introduction to performance technology* (Part 1). Washington, DC: National Society for Performance and Instruction.

Lessinger, L. M. (1970). *Every kid a winner.* New York: Simon & Schuster.

Mager, R. F. (1988). *Making instruction work: Or skillbloomers.* Belmont, CA: David S. Lake.

Mager, R. F., & Pipe, P. (1983). *CRI: Criterion referenced instruction* (2nd ed.). Carefree, AZ: Mager Associates.

Mager, R. F., & Pipe, P. (1984). *Analyzing performance problems* (2nd ed.). Belmont, CA: Pitman.

Perelman, L. J. (1989, November 28). *Closing education's technology gap* (Briefing Paper No. 111). Indianapolis, IN: Hudson Institute.

Reiser, R. A., & Gagne, R. M. (1983). *Selecting media for instruction.* Englewood Cliffs, NJ: Educational Technology.

Silvern, L. C. (1968, March). Cybernetics and education K-12. *Audiovisual Instruction.*

Stolovitch, H. D., & Keeps, E. J. (1992). *Handbook of human performance technology: A comprehensive guide for analyzing and solving performance problems in organizations.* San Francisco: Jossey-Bass (with the National Society for Performance & Instruction, Washington, DC).

Walton, M. (1986). *The Deming management method.* New York: Dodd, Mead.

Witkin, B. R. (1984). *Assessing needs in educational and social programs.* San Francisco: Jossey-Bass.

Index